CUBSESSIONS

Famous Fans of Chicago's North Side
Baseball Team and Their Stories of
Pain, Loyalty, Hope and (Finally) Joy

MARC —
2023
I HOPE YOU ENJOY THIS BOOK —
WONDERFUL STORIES & CUB DAYS
OF LORE. THANK YOU FOR ALL —
CHECK OUT PAGE 182

Becky Sarwate
AND
Randy Richardson

ECKHARTZ
PRESS

Copyright © 2019 by *Becky Sarwate* and *Randy Richardson*
Published in the United States by
Eckhartz Press
Chicago, Illinois

Cover design by *Mubasher Ashrafi*
Interior design by *Vasil Nazar*

All Rights Reserved

No part of this book may be used or reproduced in any manner whatsoever without written permission except in the case of brief quotations embodied in critical articles and reviews.

ISBN: 978-1-7336111-4-5

Dedication

For Cubs fans everywhere.
The wait was worth it.

Acknowledgements

Truth be told, this book was not our idea; credit for that goes to its publishers, Rick Kaempfer and David Stern. That they entrusted us with it we are forever thankful. This project was truly a dream come true for two die-hard Cubs fans.

To all those who shared their stories with us, we owe a debt of gratitude. Without your collective wit and wisdom and passion and patience, there would be no book. Our names are on the cover but yours fill the inside pages.

We would be remiss if we did not recognize those that carried us through this project on a personal level. There were many – too many to name them all – but here we highlight the ones that most stood out.

Randy –

One of the biggest challenges of this project was simply making connections. Along the way several people lent a helping hand. They include: Don Evans, Pat Nagle, Anthony Lewis, Janet Tabit, Yolanda Linneman and David Berner. And then there was George Rawlinson, who went above and beyond the call of duty in making three trips from the northwest suburbs to downtown Chicago to put the finishing touches on the interview with Billy Goat Tavern owner Sam Sianis. I owe all of you a beer and a cheezborger.

There's no way I could have done this project on my own. Enter Becky Sarwate, my friend and colleague who worked on it with me every step of the way. This was truly a collaborative effort and a better teammate I could not imagine.

And then finally, there are the two people to whom I am closest, my lovely wife Mitsuko, who supports my work, and my son (and future Cubs shortstop) Tyler, who inspires my work.

Becky -

This book, nay, my very writing career, would not be possible without the constant love, support and pushing of my younger sister Jennifer, who challenges me to reach the potential she's always believed I own.

My friend, colleague and fellow Cubs fan for life, Randy Richardson, has earned eternal gratitude for giving an online freelance writer with a day job the opportunity of a lifetime. Collaborating with a talented author and kindred spirit on a work of sports passion is the stuff of which bucket lists are made.

Brian Walsh is more than an assistant-of-all trades. Throughout the development of this project, he summoned an authority and confidence I didn't always feel myself, opening doors to meaningful conversations – excerpted in this book – that I will treasure for a lifetime.

Last but not least: my love, best friend, rowdiest fellow Cubs fan, gut checker and husband Bob. With this project – and for the rest of my life – you are my North Star.

Introduction

This book was very much a passion project for us. No surprise, but we are diehard Cub fans. We didn't know that when we first met. It was our deep involvement in Chicago's literary community that introduced us as colleagues, before we became friends. Eventually we came to discover a joint love of our city's North Side baseball team.

Before we share all the stories that others have told us, you should know our stories. Because they show the lenses through which we see this book and the experiences shared in it.

First up to bat, Randy:

The year I became a Cubs fan was 1969, the year of the black cat and the fabled collapse. I was in the third grade, and my family had just relocated from a suburb in Milwaukee to a south suburb of Chicago. As a newbie I didn't know about North Side-South Side allegiances and gravitated toward the Chicago team that was the more colorful of the two and, at that time, the Cubs looked like a better team to bet on that the White Sox. Because I wasn't deeply invested in the team yet, I survived that first year as a Cubs fan without any permanent scars. Those would come in due time.

In many ways, the frayed Cubs cap I wore became my identity. Everyone thought I slept in it, and I liked that they

Randy Richardson and former Cubs
third baseman Bill Madlock

saw me that way. It was who I was, an island unto myself, different from all the others around me who wore the old black and white, red and white, and for a brief time powder blue and white – the colors of the White Sox.

My first great memory of the Chicago Cubs came in 1974, a year that the franchise posted a 66-96 record to finish dead-last in the National League East. The season began with outfielder Jose Cardenal refusing to play the opener, claiming that he was injured because the eyelids of one eye were stuck open. The way the team played that year Cardenal probably wished that his eyelids had stayed glued together all-season long.

The Cubs didn't make it easy to love them that year. In the offseason and extending into the 1974 season, the team said goodbye to future Hall of Famers Fergie Jenkins, Ron Santo and Billy Williams. Fan favorites Randy Hundley and Glenn Beckert joined them out the door. Pitcher Milt Pappas retired.

Yet love them I did. While most objective baseball experts viewed the 1974 Cubs as nothing but miserable, through the lens of my 12-year-old eyes they were still something special.

Surely you can see it in the grainy, washed out photos of me with braces and long, stringy hair sticking out of my Cubs hat. This was the awkward phase that followed my parent's divorce two years earlier. The Cubs helped me through that difficult period of my life. My mom and her new boyfriend saw that and through his connection with umpire Tom Gorman, gave me the gift of a lifetime. The veteran umpire led me during pregame warmups into the Cubs' dugout, where I posed for photos with third-baseman Bill Madlock (acquired in the offseason from Texas in the Jenkins trade), utility infielder Billy Grabarkewitz, and manager Jim Marshall (who took over mid-season after the team fired Whitey Lockman).

I still have the baseball signed by many of the players. In addition to the three with whom I had photos taken, there are some memorable names on that ball: Williams (the sweet swinger, whom the team traded weeks later), Steve Stone (the pitcher who would later become a broadcaster for the Cubs and the crosstown White Sox), Rick Monday (who would gain fame two years later for what some call "the greatest play in baseball history," when he saved the American flag from being burnt by protesters while playing center field for the Cubs at Dodger Stadium), and Carmen Fanzone (a future flugelhorn player whose name the TV program *Transformers Animated* resurrected by naming a character Carmine Fanzone).

Oh, and don't let me forget Oscar Zamora, the Cubs reliever who seemed to give up a lot of hits, leading to Cubs fans making up this song, to the tune of Dean Martin's hit song "That's Amore": "When the pitch is so fat, that the ball meets the bat…that's Zamora." His name is on that ball, too.

I honestly don't even remember if the Cubs won or lost that game. It didn't really matter. They'd already won my heart.

Completing the daily-double, Becky:

Unlike my writing partner, who found his own route to Cubs fandom, I am a fourth-generation bleeder of blue. The roots run deep on both sides of my family, but the voice I hear when I yell at the TV, review lineups or go online to gape at stats is my father Gregg's. Until I met my husband Bob in early 2015, my father was the most Cubsessive person I ever knew.

Throughout my childhood, my father's perspective was the one through which I experienced the Cubs. Life with

Bob and Becky at Wrigley

dad wasn't always easy, as he suffers from a variety of mental illnesses that have nothing to do with loyalty to a historically troubled baseball franchise. But if you're bipolar, which my dad is, what could be a better match for that than being a Cubs fan? The emotional swings manifest themselves quite similarly. Much of my childhood life was ruled by my dad's moods – was it an up day (even an up day could be threatening in its own way) – or a down one? Following my dad's cycles trained me well for the highs and lows of being a Cubs fan.

During baseball season, the fortunes of the Cubs had a lot to do with which way the emotional scales tilted in our home. The first time I ever saw my father cry was in 1984. I was barely six years old, trying to understand why he was so passionate about this team while in the early stages of being sucked in myself. I experienced the collapse of the Cubs in the National League Championship Series that year with a double consciousness.

Even though we haven't spoken in years, my road with the Cubs will always run parallel to my father's. I couldn't help but think of him when the Cubs finally, at long treasured last, went all the way in 2016. And whenever they play Steve Goodman's "Go Cubs Go" at the Friendly Confines, I'm still that six-year-old dancing around the living room with her daddy.

Happily, since 2015, my husband has been more than willing to dance with me during the good times and wipe my tears when the going gets tough (I'm looking at you 2016 World Series Game 7 rain delay!). The picture you see of our two smiling faces commemorates our first trip to Wrigley Field together.

The Cubs are more than just a baseball team to those of us who have followed them through our lifetimes, from the heartache of 1969 to the pure joy of 2016. We are emotionally tied to them, much like family.

When we embarked on this book project it was the season after the Cubs had finally – gloriously – won it all. A season that saw them stumble out of the gate until they eventually found their footing to reach the postseason for the third straight year, an achievement that no other Cubs team in our lifetimes had accomplished.

Many of those interviewed are people whom we'd

followed – even idolized – from afar for years. What we came to find is that we are all one. No matter how divergent our life paths, the roads that we've taken, the failures that we've experienced, or the successes that we've reached, we all share this one common bond: the Chicago Cubs.

The stories of how we all came together to share this one collective passion are what make us all unique.

Some didn't start out as Cubs fans at all. Former major league pitcher Steve Trout began as a White Sox fan. Mystery author Sara Paretsky's team was the old Kansas City Athletics. Rock radio deejay Lin Brehmer cheered for the New York Yankees in his youth. Yet their career paths all led them to the Cubs. As Brehmer explained: "…when I fell for the Chicago Cubs I fell hard."

Others were born and raised with the Cubbie blue running through their veins. Legal thriller author Scott Turow is a third-generation Cubs fan. NPR's Scott Simon's godfather was Jack Brickhouse, the former Cubs broadcaster. For actor-comedian Nick Offerman, Cubs games were the main household entertainment all through childhood.

Whether they are famous for acting, joke-telling, broadcasting, writing, cooking, pitching, or cheering, when you peel away those tags for which they are best known, they are just like me and you – the readers of this book. They are Cubs fans.

1. Jonathan Alter

Journalist, best-selling author, and television producer Jonathan Alter worked for *Newsweek* magazine for nearly 20 years beginning in the early 1980s. Since 1996, he's been a contributing correspondent to NBC News, and has appeared on the NBC, MSNBC, and CNBC networks. One might think the wizened reporter has seen it all. Yet the Chicago Cubs World Series win in 2016 had Alter feeling like a kid again.

"Needless to say I was excited," he said via telephone interview. "My son [television producer] Tommy and I went to the three games that were in Chicago. Credentials let us go onto the field. We spoke to [Cubs pitching great] Fergie Jenkins before one of the games, which was wonderful for me. We were so glad to be there. I didn't make the parade but I did go to five of the seven total Series games."

For a detached reporter who happens to be a diehard fan, the magical night of November 2, 2016, when the Cubs finally won it all, was something special.

"I promised myself I'd go to Game 7 with a press pass if it happened. My son couldn't go with me. But I got there early. I wanted to see if I could get a special pass for the clubhouse post-game celebration if there was to be one. I was turned down.

"I watched most of the game from the press box, but

eventually made my way down to some seats behind home plate. I watched the last four innings and rain delay with my nephew. We shared this moment of pure bliss when they won. We will never see a game as good. We were witnessing a piece of history."

Then came the utter pandemonium that ensued after Rizzo pocketed the game-winning ball. "I raced down toward the field, but there were so many people I couldn't get there. A friendly Cleveland security guard let me walk across the Indians dugout to get to the field. It was thrilling. I almost ran into Rizzo, who was still holding the ball. Everyone was hugging and smiling. I saw John Cusack, whom I'd profiled in *Esquire* years ago. We bear-hugged and then I did the same with Bill Murray. And because I was now with Cusack, I was able to get into the dugout.

"When I got there, there's David Ross sitting on the bench. He'd just become the oldest player to ever hit a home run in the World Series. I started babbling – all my memories and what this meant to me. Babbling like an idiot. Ross looks at me, stands up and says, 'You deserve a hug too.' I'll never forget the sweet smell of his uniform. The sense of wonder and exhilaration. It's beyond imagining."

Like many thunderstruck fans, Jonathan Alter knew he'd have trouble going to sleep that night. Goodwill was prevalent and contagious.

"I was there long after other reporters had left. The

players and management could have shooed me away politely, but none of them did that. I have this vivid memory of Kyle Schwarber with his sister and niece, and he's playing hide-and-go-seek with the kid. I watched and waited until the game was over. It was so cute. He's a good egg. There are so many variables involved in what makes a team win. These guys had good chemistry. They had one of the greatest managers ever. And they liked each other. That's so important."

Alter has been around long enough to draw upon ready examples of Cubs teams past where the chemistry was decidedly off. The journalist was born in Chicago in 1957 and followed the franchise through tough decades. Raised in a Jewish family in a home less than a mile from Wrigley Field, Alter grew up cheering for both Windy City baseball clubs. "My father was a lifelong Cubs fan," he said. "But my mother's father was a Sox fan and would take me to their games. In that era, there was no shame in rooting for both teams. That became unfashionable later."

The self-proclaimed "Jewish left-hander" recalled a particularly exciting game he attended on September 25, 1966. "My father took me to see the Cubs' Kenny Holtzman pitch against the Dodgers' Sandy Koufax. Two Jewish left-handers in the same game! It was a very cold day, and unbelievably both pitchers had no-hitters going into the late innings. In the end the Cubs beat Koufax. It was a very sweet and memorable moment for me."

Oftentimes, young Alter would go to games unattended. From 1967 to 1972, the boy walked to "dozens" of games each year. "We lived so close to Wrigley. My parents believed in giving kids freedom and responsibility at an early age. No coddling. I would do chores in the morning and then my mother would send me off with a packed brown bag lunch, a dollar for admission to the bleachers, and maybe another dollar for frosty malts and peanuts.

"I'd get to the park about 11 a.m., sit in the bleachers and watch the Cubs take batting practice. It was heaven. I'd watch until 1:15 p.m., which was game time. I liked sitting in left field, which is where the Bleacher Bums were born. I learned a lot from them. I was partly raised by the original Bleacher Bums – a great assortment of characters. For five years, Wrigley Field was my summer home.

"The 1967 team record is the exact opposite record of the 2016 record. Most days that I went to games, the Cubs would lose, but I didn't seem to mind. I was having too much fun."

Alter admitted that winning is pretty enjoyable too, particularly after such a long and emotional wait. Ultimately, what does the 2016 World Series mean to the embedded journalist?

"The curse is lifted, and Game 7 had everything," he said. "The Cubs took it to the level of possibly the greatest baseball game ever played. You can definitely quote me on that."

2. Ike Barinholtz

Ike Barinholtz was probably only five years old the first time he stepped into the Friendly Confines. But it made a lasting impression.

"I went to my first game – I want to say it was about 1982 – and I remember walking in the ballpark – and I swear that Dickie Noles was the pitcher that day," Barinholtz said in a phone interview. "I just remember being blown away and loving it."

The following year, the Barinholtz family picked up and moved from Rogers Park to Lake View, around Irving Park and Clarendon, about a half mile from Wrigley Field. Barinholtz was only seven when the Cubs, led by future Hall of Famer Ryne Sandberg and pitcher Rick Sutcliffe, won the National League's Eastern Division in 1984, to reach the postseason for the first time since 1945. They went up 2-0 in the best-of-five National League Championship Series against the Padres only to lose the next three games in San Diego.

Barinholtz, who had a recurring role as car thief-turned-nurse Morgan Tookers on the hit Hulu comedy series *The Mindy Project* and has starred in several movies including *Neighbors*, and its sequel, *Neighbors 2: Sorority Rising*, *Sisters*, and *Suicide Squad*, learned the first hard lesson of what it meant to be a Cub fan when the ball rolled through first baseman Leon Durham's legs in Game 5 of that 1984 series.

"I remember it as clear as day," Barinholtz said, "sitting in my parents' living room, I was watching it on TV and just not understanding it. To see them lose to San Diego…it was heartbreaking. But it's good if you experience trauma at an early age. Because then if it happens throughout your life, you should be more prepared for it."

Barinholtz's father, Alan Barinholtz, an attorney, is the rare breed of Chicagoan who roots for both the North Side Cubs and the South Side Sox. "There's a small subsect of people who are both Cubs fans and Sox fans," Ike explained. "I kind of fall under that in the sense that I'm happy when the Sox do well. But I will always root for the Cubs. My ultimate scenario would be to see the Cubs and the Sox go to the World Series and for the Cubs to beat them in four games and throw four perfect games. For the White Sox, it would be nice enough for them to get there."

The elder Barinholtz taught the son about the pain and suffering that came with being a Cubs fan – from the Cubs' infamous trade of future Hall of Famer Lou Brock to the St. Louis Cardinals for pitcher Ernie Broglio, to the team's epic collapse in 1969. "From very early on," Barinholtz said, "the mythology and the pain that comes with being a Cubs fan was instilled in my brain."

Through all the years of losing, Barinholtz said, "abandoning [the Cubs] was never an option." As he explained: "It's the same thing that makes up a good marriage: loyalty and patience. You just had to wait much, much, much longer for the ring. I felt like a girl who's been waiting so long and all the friends keep asking, 'When is he going to put a ring on it?' Now I've got this giant ring and all my friends are jealous."

Before he got the ring, as fate would have it, Barinholtz had to suffer a little bit more. "I was in LA," Barinholtz said. "I knew that if [the Cubs] got to the World Series, there was no way that I wasn't going to go to Chicago. I would have done anything to get a ticket, and I ended up getting tickets to Games 4 and 5. I went with my wife to Game 4, which we lost. Then we were out that night and I wasn't feeling well. I was supposed to go to that next game with my dad, and the Cubs had two tickets for me. At like noon, my dad looked at me and said, 'There's something wrong with you.' I had a hundred and three temperature. I had the worst flu and I could not go to Game 5, which is the night that they turned everything around."

Still recovering from his bout with the flu, Barinholtz had to pass on an invite to join his friends at the Village Idiots, a Cub-friendly bar in Los Angeles. "My wife tells me, 'If you go, you will die.' So I watched Game 7 in pajamas with tissues all around me and I watched it with my wife and a friend of mine. When they won, it was like in *Hoosiers* when they cut to Dennis Hopper in the hospital. He's like screaming and jumping up and down and he's hugging the nurses. That's what I felt like. I was crying. It was this feeling of contentedness. I called all of my Cubs friends and we all cried. Even my wife, who is more of a Sox fan, was crying. It was the greatest. It was surreal."

On a Sunday afternoon in mid-May, with the Cubs squaring off against division rival Milwaukee Brewers, Barinholtz finally made it back to the Friendly Confines, where he threw out the first pitch and led the seventh-inning stretch in singing "Take Me Out to the Ball Game." The Cubs went on to win that game 13-6, belting out four home runs. For Barinholtz, that's when he really took it all in.

"There are certain things in life that are not like things that are not necessarily weighing you down but they're things that are on your mind and you always wonder 'What will happen with this?'" Barinholtz said. "One of the things that had been weighing on me was 'Are the Cubs ever going to win?' And the reason it was weighing on me was that my dad assumed that they would win in his lifetime and his dad assumed that they would win in his lifetime. Having them win now hasn't diminished my fandom at all, it's just taken that stress or unsatisfying aspect and made it gratifying. Basically, it's just one less thing that I can worry about. Now I can watch them stress-free and enjoy them for what they are."

3. Lin Brehmer

For Lin Brehmer, it has always been about baseball.

"I grew up at a time in America where you ate breakfast, which was sadly something like Corn Flakes, and then you walked out of the house with your glove and maybe a bat that had been dropped on concrete playgrounds so much that the part of the bat at the end that is supposed to hold your grip has already disappeared and chipped away," Brehmer said in a telephone interview. "And then you found your friends and you played baseball for the next ten hours. By baseball, I mean baseball, stickball, fast pitch, stoop ball, punch ball, softball, baseball with a tennis ball – anything that involved a ball and catching and throwing and hitting. I did that everyday every summer for as long as I was a kid."

In some sense, the legendary rock DJ for Chicago's WXRT, has never really grown up. He certainly has gotten older but he maintains that heart of a kid. And baseball – along with music – keeps that heart pumping.

These days, it's the Cubs. But back when he was a kid growing up in New York, it was more about the Yankees. But then, it was more about the sport of baseball than about any individual team. And the Cubs were a big part of his life, so much so that he and his playground friends became the founding members of the Cleo James Fan Club, a small but passionate following for an obscure outfielder who played for the Cubs between 1970 and 1973, compiling a career .228 batting average with five home runs and 27 RBI. Hanging from Brehmer's office door is a placard commemorating his title as "Founding Member and President for Life of the Cleo James Fan Club" on which it reads of James: "He won some, he lost some, but he suited up for them all."

Brehmer, who began working professionally in radio in 1977 as a disc jockey in Albany, New York, at WQBK-FM, where he earned the nickname, "The Reverend of Rock and Roll," credits his passion for baseball for playing a big role in his being hired to work for WXRT as music director beginning in October 1984. At the time, Norm Winer was program director and a die-hard Cub fan.

"For our interview, we ate Chicago pizza, drank beer and watched a Cubs-Mets game," Brehmer recalled. "One of the reasons I think I got this job – one of the reasons I'm in Chicago – is that I could talk about baseball with him every step of the way. If I didn't have a fundamental grounding in the history of baseball, there's no way I'd be sitting here at WXRT talking to you today."

Winer sealed the deal with Brehmer, who had been simultaneously offered a job at an alternative rock station in Long Island, New York, by promising to take him to see the Cubs play in the World Series, if they made it that far. "I was already anticipating moving to Chicago and immediately going to see the Cubs play in the World Series…well, we all know how that worked out. It worked out badly."

The Cubs, after winning the first two games of the National League Championship Series against the San Diego Padres, lost three straight games in San Diego. The dream of the Cubs playing in their first World Series since 1945 had died. "That Sunday, I arrived in the rain," Brehmer said. "It was bad for all kinds of reasons. The next year, there I was standing in line for Opening Day tickets. And by 1989, I was a season ticket holder and have been ever since."

That was the start of his love affair with the Chicago Cubs. "The whole game of baseball has deepened its importance in my emotional life so much over the years, that when I fell for the Chicago Cubs I fell hard," Brehmer said. "The Chicago Cubs are the centerpiece of my spring and summer, and from the time I fell in love with the Chicago Cubs, I've put a giant 'X' on my desk calendar through the month of October in the hopes that that month is not available for anything else.

"The Cubs are the source of so much joy and so much pain. They've really been one of the most important parts of my adult life and of my family's life. If the Cubs are on TV, my wife [Sara Farr] and my son [Wilson], if he's around, we're watching it. I can't turn away and I can't turn away an opportunity to go to a game when I have a clearing in my schedule. As I say to my closest friends, who understand, 'With regards to the Chicago Cubs, I kind of have a problem.' Love is not rational. You can't say, 'Oh, you're in love, this makes sense.' Very little about love makes sense in the traditional sense."

At the outset of the 2016 baseball season, Brehmer, in his Lin's Bin radio commentary, dared to broach the question: What if?

He wrote: "The prophets have warned us that when the Cubs win, the world will not be able to stem the tide of global doom. As any extreme mountain climber can tell you, the danger is not in reaching the summit of Everest, the danger is coming down. Do we really want the Cubs to win the World Series?"

In Nostradamus-like fashion, he may have predicted what was to come. Because he answered his question this way: "Allow us the shortness of breath that comes from reaching the greatest height. And if we end the season with the Cubs in 7, I promise we will breathe again because we will no longer be holding our breath."

The roller-coaster ride that was the 2016 postseason "nearly destroyed" him in an emotional sense. When it came down to Game 7 of the World Series, Brehmer was at a watch party with his wife and his son and his closest friends, including Winer and his other XRT colleagues, Wendy Rice and Marty Lennartz – his "Chicago Cubs family." As Brehmer emphasized, "There were no casual fans there."

When Rajai Davis belted that game-tying two-run home run in the bottom of the eighth, Brehmer said, "There was a darkness that settled over the room." As Brehmer explained: "We were all together in the failures of 2007 and 2008 and 1998 and 1989. They were of course very much present in the summer of '84 and '69. All that accumulated horror came to rest over us like a cloud. Some people walked downstairs to be alone in rooms. Some people just sat there with their heads in their hands. I didn't know if any of us were going to be able to pull out of that feeling. Then it started to rain."

Brehmer had to be on the air first thing the next morning. Expecting a long rain delay, "I stood up and I said, 'I love you all, but I've got to go home.'"

He drove home alone, leaving his family behind. And so, sitting alone in the same room where he'd watched Cubs games for the last quarter century, he watched the Cubs come back after the rain delay to pull it out and win their first championship since 1908. "When they won, I leaped up, arms in the air, shouting like I was in a crowded bar," he said, "then I looked around me and I realized, 'Who are you doing that for? You're all by yourself.'"

After all the inevitable celebratory phone calls and texts, Brehmer took a moment of private celebration. "I thought to myself, 'I should have a big tumbler of my best bourbon on the rocks or maybe tequila.' I'm going back and forth and I thought, 'No, no, no, no – that's all wrong. You feel like an 8-year-old right now. What you need is a root beer float.' So I watched the post-game sitting in my comfy chair with a big smile on my face spooning a root beer float into my mouth."

True to his promise, he breathed again.

> "When it comes to favorite Cubs songs I can never pick just one. The one until they won the pennant was a Chicago singer-songwriter by the name of Jeff Boyle, who did a song called 'Cubs Win.' It's on YouTube. Listen to it. It's awesome.
>
> "The one I loved after they won was a song written by a guy who used to be a Chicago resident, Ted Wulfers. He played in clubs around Chicago for years. He moved out west somewhere but he kept following the Cubs. I think it was two days after the Cubs won the World Series he sent me a copy of a song. It's called 'The Cubs Won It All in 2016.' It's a pretty simple song. Acoustic guitar. He writes, 'I wrote this song around 3 a.m. on November 3 after watching the Cubs win the 2016 World Series. Holy Cow. I hope this song brings a smile and tear and warms the hearts as much as it was writing about this epic and historic event.' I heard it and I went to my bosses and I said, 'We've got to play this,' and we played it a bunch and it got back to Ted and it got out there in the ether of social media and the Baseball Hall of Fame asked him for a printout of the lyrics to the song. To this day 'The Cubs Won it all in 2016' by Ted Wulfers is ensconced somewhere in Cooperstown.
>
> "And of course the third best Cubs song is Eddie Vedder's 'All the Way.' When we do our WXRT

Opening Day celebration, it's a standard; we always play it. It has kind of a different caste to it now that the Cubs have won, but it is always to me one of the better Irish drinking songs."

— Lin Brehmer

4. Pat Brickhouse

Loyal April pilgrims to Wrigley Field know that Chicago winters often overstay their welcome. It's not unusual to see fans in down jackets and/or wrapped in blankets at the Cubs home opener, and into the spring. Chicago is a tough city made more resilient by the harsh challenges of short days and brutal winds. Diminutive yet vigorous, Pat Brickhouse – widow of broadcasting legend Jack – has a special place in her heart for those chilly early-season games.

"Jack and I were not married yet and it was in the late 1970s," she recalled during a phone conversation. "My earliest Wrigley remembrance is being there while snowflakes were falling. They were so big, I was able to differentiate them. That experience stays with me."

Brickhouse has always been an interesting mix of poet and tomboy, perhaps the secret sauce that first drew Jack to the Omaha, Nebraska, native. Pat proudly described a girlhood enmeshed with sports. "I was an only child, born when both of my parents were in their 40s," she said. "I always tell people that marrying Jack Brickhouse was one of the easiest things I ever did because I was the son my parents never had. My dad was an All-American basketball player. He took his little girl to all the games and matches. My mother wanted no part of it. We'd drop her off at the movies."

Sometimes Brickhouse found herself straddling the lines

between spectator and participant. She recalled attending a boxing match with her father as a young girl. "I was eight years old and we were sitting in the front row," she said. "Picture me with long Shirley Temple curls, which were very chic in those days. Suddenly everyone hears yours-truly screaming at the top of her lungs. There was a strong punch and a boxer's mouthpiece landed right in my lap. Rather than coddle me, my dad was so embarrassed that he dragged me out of the venue."

Pat Brickhouse is disarmingly humble, a great storyteller who genuinely loves sports, her late husband and a good cocktail. Though Jack Brickhouse passed away nearly 20 years ago, she gently ribbed him about pedestrian drink tastes as if he were in the next room. She deadpanned, "Jack was a scotch man. He would buy Chivas Regal if he felt extra flush with cash."

A natural enthusiasm for life and competition rendered the Brickhouses perfect companions. "Jack loved to work," she said. "He would overlap the Cubs and the Bears seasons. Double- and sometimes triple-duty when he'd cross town to announce White Sox games. He was the first televised voice of the Chicago Bulls. We traveled all over, East Coast to West Coast, energized by Chicago sports fans – the greatest in the world. But Jack also enjoyed other types of work. He interviewed the Pope. He loved doing man-on-the-street reports. He loved people."

Although Jack Brickhouse lent his vocal talents to nearly every Windy City sporting franchise at one time or another, his longest tenure was with the Cubs organization. From 1941 to 1945, and again from 1948 to 1981, no Cubbies win was complete without the enthusiastic "Hey! Hey!" that ended the broadcast.

"What it means for me is what it meant to Jack," she reflected. "He had such incredible optimism, broadcasting for the team throughout all those losing years. He coined the phrase 'the Loveble Losers.' He had such affection for the loyal fans who always kept hope alive.

"People would ask Jack, 'How are the Cubs going to do next year?' Finally, in 1978 he developed a perfect answer, 'Anyone can have a bad century.' Little did he realize it would take eight years longer than a century. But the dream finally came to fruition."

Pat Brickhouse's long reign as the First Lady of the Chicago Cubs underscores the emotional ride and lasting impact of the 2016 season. During the painfully suspenseful final game of the World Series, Brickhouse was one with other vigilant, silently pleading, fans. "I was biting my nails during Game 7 and the rain delay," she said. "I didn't travel. The last thing I wanted was to get entangled in those crowds."

With each shift in momentum, she thought of the man who so loved the team and its fans. "He always said, 'Maybe someday I'll have to go to work for a living.' He never thought of what he did as labor. Jack got his start in radio in the 1930s at 18 years old. At that time, he was the youngest broadcaster in the nation. After an internship in New York that he called the worst year of his life, Jack came to Chicago and never wanted to leave."

Brickhouse may have died in 1998, but his wish to remain in the Windy City is fully realized. A memorial statue of the broadcasting legend erected in 2000 keeps company with Michigan Avenue residents and tourists. The bust was a significant landmark along the Cubs World Series 2016 parade route.

Fans who attend Cubs games at Wrigley Field today can't help but notice the "Hey! Hey!" markers on the foul poles. And in the summer of 2017, the Budweiser Brickhouse Tavern opened its doors as part of the Ricketts Park at Wrigley community project. Pat Brickhouse was intimately involved in the restaurant's creation. "Jack had a lot of opportunities and backers during his lifetime who advocated for a restaurant. But he knew what he didn't know. He didn't want to be associated with failure. He would be so proud to be a part of this venture now – and of what his team finally accomplished."

Hey! Hey!

5. Dave Cihla

Dave Cihla and his bleacher buddies first raised the Shawon-O-Meter in the left field bleachers of Wrigley Field in a game against the New York Mets on June 5, 1989. The makeshift placard displayed the batting average of the Cubs shortstop, the rifle-armed Shawon Dunston, followed by the words "And rising!!!"

From that initial series in June of 1989, the Shawon-O-Meter followed the Cubs shortstop through the 90s, as Dunston was traded to San Francisco in 1995 and then back to the Cubs for the 1996 season. His last season was 2002 with the Giants. Cihla and his buddies brought the Shawon-O-Meter to several games at Wrigley when Shawon was on opposing teams, usually to the grumblings of a few Cubs fans.

Original versions of the Shawon-O-Meter are stored in the archives of the Smithsonian Institution, Baseball Hall of Fame and Chicago History Museum. Now one of those signs is featured in a display case showcasing Cubs photos and memorabilia underneath the left field bleachers, below where the Shawon-O-Meter's remarkable journey all began.

By day, Cihla, the man behind "the Meter," is a mild-mannered real estate broker, married with a teenage daughter who is touring college campuses. Not exactly what you expect when you see him stand up in the crowd, raise the Meter over his head and yell at the top of his lungs, "Let's go, Shawon! Shawon-O-Meter! Yeah!"

But then Cihla, and his bleacher mates, who included Mindy Lehman and Jim Cybul, were largely anonymous figures to the fixture that the Meter had become.

"I think that was the beauty of the Meter," Cihla wrote in response to an email interview. "We were stewards that had to be there and were honored to be part of almost every broadcast when the Meter was in the bleachers and opposing team's venues. It was great fun letting other fans hold up the Meter and sharing the excitement."

Cihla has been a Cub fan as long as he can remember. "I have pictures of myself when I was in kindergarten wearing a Cubs uniform," he said during an interview in the Wrigley Field bleachers. "When I was in kindergarten my dad told me, 'We're going to get you a Cubs uniform today,' and it was, at that point, the happiest day of my life. I wore it to school the next day."

Cihla credits his bleacher buddy Cybul with coming up with the idea for the Shawon-O-Meter. "We were looking to create a sign that would get noticed on TV and Dunston's average had just dropped to .203," Cihla recalled. "We did it for four games against the Mets in June of '89. By the end, it was just trashed because it had been raining, so we just left it behind. Almost two months later, I'm watching a game in August and Harry Caray says, 'Where are those Shawon-O-

Meter guys? We need them back in the bleachers!' I called Jim immediately and we made a sturdier version this time. From that point on, we made it to every game that year."

Of the Shawon-O-Meter's popularity, Cihla said: "I think it was a unique sign, changing daily with running commentary at the bottom. And it helped that Shawon went from .203 at the start to an ending 1989 average of .278."

Cihla looks back nostalgically at that time of his life. "So much happened in that compressed period, and it was a time of relative delinquency," he wrote in an email. "But it was also a time of incredible excitement and possibility that could not have been bested but with a trip to the World Series. Those days seemed carefree, even though we had jobs and responsibilities but somehow managed to get the Meter in the bleachers most days."

In 2016, a quarter century later, Cihla was back with a new hand-made sign, the Schwarb-O-Meter, which tracks outfielder Kyle Schwarber's slugging percentage. He brought it to all four games that the Cubs played in Cleveland during the 2016 World Series, raising it above his head every time the young slugger stepped to the plate. Schwarber miraculously had come back from a torn ACL in his left knee suffered in game 3 of the season to be the Cubs' designated hitter in the championship series. Schwarber cemented legendary status by hitting safely in all four games as DH, going 7-for-17 (.412 batting average), including 3-for-5 in Game 7.

Being there at Game 7 goes down there with those moments in your life where you literally had to pinch yourself, said Cihla, who had bought a ticket for $600 and, in the seventh inning, moved to the left field bleachers, where a friend had somehow found four open seats. "I felt like I was back home in Wrigley," Cihla said. "It felt like this was where I needed to be for these final innings."

With the second out in the bottom of the tenth inning, Cihla said, "I literally had to remind myself to breathe at that moment. I'd never felt that before."

At the last out, his cell phone battery was down to about two percent power, but he had just enough left to capture that last out and then he stood there and scanned the crowd. "Men were just openly weeping," he said. "I had never seen anything like it in my life."

6. Grant DePorter

The superstitions of sports fans are a fairly sacred, if misunderstood, phenomenon. In May of 2012, *Bleacher Report* published a list of "Baseball's 50 Weirdest All-Time Superstitions." Number two on that list belongs to Moises Alou, an infamous outfielder who played three seasons with the Chicago Cubs (2002-2004). Eschewing batting gloves, Alou was known to urinate on his hands in an effort to toughen them. While this ritual may have disgusted some, the player's lifetime .303 career batting average and 332 home runs point – at the very least – to a form of psychological effectiveness.

You won't find Grant DePorter, President and Managing Partner of Harry Caray's Restaurant Group, deriding Alou – or anyone else – for a tendency to find cause and effect in unusual places. In fact, DePorter gained national attention in 2004 for a high-profile act of bad mojo exorcism. He blew up "the Bartman ball" in front of American television audiences, paying $113,824.16 to allow every member of Cubs Nation to witness the end of the ultimate symbol of franchise defeat. The aforementioned Moises Alou had a lot to do with the channeling of rage toward the ball and its namesake during and after Game 6 of the 2003 National League Championship Series. Alou, the Cubs' leftfielder in that game, thought he had a play on the ball and reacted (some would argue overreacted) by slamming his glove down in anger and frustration. In DePorter's mind, the relationship makes perfect sense, as everything in the Cubs universe is connected.

DePorter's Cubsession – and the awareness of patterns that seem to pop up everywhere – began during a particularly inauspicious year for the team. His father Donald's hospitality career moved the family to Chicago in 1969, and the young boy's life was changed forever.

"My dad started with Hyatt hotels when there were just a few of them in America," DePorter shared during a telephone interview. "He opened the Hyatt Regency O'Hare, and while that project was underway, he took me to my first game at Wrigley Field. I was probably five years old. I didn't see much of the action because the Cubs were doing so well that everyone was standing. So my dad explained to me what was going on."

The famous *Eloise* children's book series, written by Kay Thompson in the 1950s, detailed the adventures of a little girl living in a "room on the tippy-top floor" of the Plaza Hotel. The beloved series could have been franchised into a Chicago edition featuring the young Grant – with some baseball celebrity thrown into the mix. "I lived in a hotel for a lot of my childhood," DePorter recalled, "so many players would come through and I had the chance to meet them. I met Hank Aaron. The Cubs convention first started at the

Hyatt Regency Chicago in 1986. Those gatherings exposed me to the team in a really special way. When you meet the players and know them a bit, you're more invested in the team overall. I was a lucky kid."

As he grew into an adult, DePorter became so invested in Cubs history and lore that in 2008, he revived the team's first notable fan club, the West Side Rooters. The Rooters were originally founded in 1908 by legendary Cubs shortstop Joe Tinker (of the famed double play trio Tinker, Evers and Chance). The relaunch of the Rooters was the result of more than simple fan loyalty. For DePorter, it was another talisman needed to combat many decades of bad Cubs energy. After all, the Rooters were disbanded after the Cubs won the World Series in 1908, and the team hadn't stepped on a championship game field since.

There was solid precedent to support DePorter's belief that getting the club back together might pay off. "In 2004, when the Boston Red Sox won the Series, the team gave credit to the return [of their own fan club] the Royal Rooters," DePorter said. "JFK's grandfather Honey Fitzgerald was an original chair of Boston's Rooters. They brought them back in 2004, and lo and behold the team won. Why couldn't it be the same for us?"

Though the return on investment for rebooting the West Side Rooters was not immediate, lasting eight full seasons before a World Series trophy finally came to Wrigley Field,

DePorter is convinced that it was a necessary element. Somewhat akin to burning sage for two leap years.

Superstitions are a way of synthesizing the unexplainable, finding order and logic as a coping mechanism that can bring communities together. Grant DePorter's high-profile and prolific sharing of noticeable patterns throughout Cubs history has rendered him a sort of folk hero amongst his fellow fans.

"*USA Today* put me on its cover in 2004 for blowing up the Bartman ball," he explained. "Following the story, people started sending me their own patterns.

"In 2016, I went over the list with Anthony Rizzo. Addison Russell saw me on ESPN talking about it at around the same time. Separately, I made the news in Cleveland. A lot of people were buzzing about it there. Maybe I had something to do with reinforcing a mental edge for the Cubs. If you believe in a higher power or supernatural forces…well that's how it played out for me."

Though a World Series Championship finally came to the North Side of Chicago in 2016, DePorter remains a staunch believer in numbers and patterns. His new favorite digit is '2'. Before the start of the 2017 season he "invited 80 identical twin Cub fans to a rally to create some positive energy," he said. "It was a play on Ernie Banks' legendary words – 'Let's play two!'"

The only thing more enjoyable than one Cubs World

Series is a repeat.

> "Three numbers and a name encompass basically all of Cubs history – 8, 13, 108, and Murphy. I figured it would take the Cubs 108 years to win another World Series, especially when 2008 wasn't the year. 108 is everywhere that's good for the Cubs. City of Chicago plan development number 108 belongs to Wrigley Field. 2016 ace pitcher John Lester born in Tacoma, Washington, the 108th largest city in America. And the Ricketts family headquarters are located – where else? – on 108th Avenue in Omaha."
>
> — Grant DePorter

7. Tom Dreesen

Legendary comedian Tom Dreesen grew up in Harvey, Illinois, a south suburb of Chicago, where his allegiance to the North Side Cubs didn't always make him popular.

"Growing up, as a little boy, my dad listened to Cubs games on the radio, and I had an uncle who also listened to Cubs games," Dreesen said during a phone interview from his home in Southern California. "So I was a Cub fan at about five years old, not realizing that I lived in enemy territory. So I always say that by the time I was eight years old, I could take a punch. Because all around me were Sox fans."

Dreesen, now 78, never shied away from being different. In 1968, while working as an insurance salesman, he met Tim Reid through a local Jaycee chapter, and the two teamed up as Tim and Tom, the first biracial stand-up comedy duo in the United States. Though their material is now considered cutting-edge for its time, the pair struggled to make a living together and split up in the mid-1970s. However, each found unlikely success on their own: while Reid gained fame playing deejay Venus Flytrap on the sitcom *WKRP in Cincinnati*, Dreesen became a regular on late night TV, first on *The Tonight Show* starring Johnny Carson and then on *Late Night* with David Letterman. But he's perhaps best known for hanging out with many of Hollywood's biggest names and most notably his close friendship with legendary singer Frank Sinatra. He was the crooner's opening act for 14 years, the master of ceremonies at his wake and one of the pallbearers at his funeral.

Through all of the Hollywood successes Dreesen never forgot where he came from and never stopped rooting for his favorite baseball team. In 1982, he became the first president of the Die-Hard Cub Fan's Club. Then in 1987, at age 47, he served as the Cubs' honorary bat boy during day games before performing his late-night comedy shows at Zanie's. "I'd suit up and they let me hit batting practice and run around the outfield and catch fly balls," Dreesen recalled. "I was in hog heaven."

One day while on duty as bat boy he turned the tables on Cubs pitcher Rick Sutcliffe's practical joke. Sutcliffe, nicknamed "The Red Baron" for his red hair and beard, prodded Dreesen to compliment home plate umpire Frank Pulli. As Dreesen tells the story, Sutcliffe said, "When you go out to pick up the bat, tell Frank that I think he's the best umpire in the National League." So Dreesen tries to do just that as the umpire was dusting off home plate but before he could even get to the compliment, Pulli turned red and erupted with a flurry of profanities. "I don't give a f- what Rick Sutcliffe said. And I don't give a f- what you have to say. Pick up the f-ing bats and go back to the dugout. You're a bat boy.

"Now I realize that [Sutcliffe] set me up," Dreesen said.

"So I go back to the dugout and he asks me what he said, and I told him that he told me to tell you that he thinks you're the best pitcher in both leagues."

The lesson: don't try to pull a joke on a professional jokester. He'll always turn the joke back on you.

But the comic turns serious when you ask him what the Cubs have meant to him. "I live in a world where I'm in and out of airplanes, flying here and there, to Iraq and back, performing for the troops. I toured for 14 years as the opening act for Frank Sinatra. All of us, at some point, subconsciously wish that time would stand still and that's what happens when you go into a ballpark and you sit in a seat that your great-grandfather sat in, that your grandfather sat in, that your father sat in, that you sat in, that your son sat in, that your son's son will sit in. They're all going to watch that same game, and, for just a moment, time stands still. That can only happen at Wrigley Field. It's my childhood. Look, I'm in my 70s, and I'm still that same little boy that walked into Wrigley Field for his very first time."

For the 2016 World Series, Dreesen attended all three games played at Wrigley Field. The Cubs lost the first two but won Game 5 to send the Series back to Cleveland. Dreesen had to return to Southern California for a show. He had a suite at the Marriott Palm Desert, which incidentally is the place where Frank Sinatra sang his last song. It was Game 7 and, like every Cub fan, he was a bundle of nerves.

"When they won – I make my living, for almost 50 years now, speaking on stage – I was absolutely speechless. The phone was ringing. Every Cubs fan I knew was trying to call me, but I couldn't answer the phone because I couldn't talk. My daughter called, and I tried to talk to her and I couldn't talk. I walked the floor, tears coming down my face. I just kept thinking about all those years – the jokes we took, the ragging and the jokes, and the curse and the goat. It's over. It's finally over. It was just hard to believe."

8. Dennis Franz

Growing up in Maywood, west of Chicago, in the 1950s, Dennis Franz's sport was baseball and his team was the Cubs. Not surprisingly, his favorite player was No. 14, Ernie Banks (aka "Mr. Cub").

"He was my hero," Franz said in a phone interview. "I grew up trying to bat like him, wiggling my fingers like him…"

Two decades later, Franz was a budding actor in Chicago perfecting his craft in the Organic Theater Company, a repertory theater that had set up shop in the Uptown Center Hull House on Beacon Street. The new company, which also included Joe Mantegna and Meshach Taylor, gained some notoriety in 1974, when it presented the world premiere of *Sexual Perversity in Chicago* by David Mamet.

Two years later, Mantegna planted the seed for a play about Cub fans. "[Mantegna] would walk by [Wrigley Field] every day and he'd see all these fans spilling out of the stadium," Franz said, and he thought, 'There's got to be some way to bring them into our theater.'"

[Mantegna's] the one that brought the idea and got us thinking in that direction," Franz said. "Collectively, we all started talking about it and we decided we'd start going to some of the games to try to find some interesting people. So that was our homework. When we weren't performing, we'd go to Wrigley and we'd watch the games and look for interesting characters. We came to see this little group in the bleachers that were always there, and they were interesting and fun people and bets were flying around. There was just a lot going on."

Those real-life characters became the inspiration for *Bleacher Bums*, which debuted in 1977 under the direction of Stuart Gordon. "We decided it was going to be one game that was representative of the heartbreak that was experienced by the Cubs over the years on a regular basis," Franz said. "How the hopes get built up and dreams are crashed and still you remain a loyal Cubs fan."

Bleacher Bums and its themes of hope, futility and – most of all – die-hard loyalty, struck a chord and toured across the country with changing casts that included Dennis Farina, Gary Sandy and George Wendt. A 1979 performance of the play was taped for PBS television, and in 2002, a made-for-TV movie adaptation was produced.

As it turned out, *Bums* was Franz's final show with the Organic Theater Company before he hitched up a U-Haul and headed for Hollywood. "I think we all were kind of surprised by the popularity of it," Franz said. "Quite honestly, I didn't think it was our best work. But it turned out to be one of the most beloved works that we had done over that five-year period and for those of us who worked on the original production, it certainly has the fondest place in all of our hearts. We just wanted to fill the seats of the theater and it turned into this thing that I think everyone of us is grateful for."

In Hollywood, Franz gained fame for his tough-but-lovable cop roles, first as Lt. Norman Buntz on *Hill Street Blues* and later as Detective Andy Sipowicz on *NYPD Blue*, for which he earned four Emmy Awards for Outstanding Lead Actor in a Drama Series.

Before he landed those star-making roles, Franz played pitching coach Angelo Carbone in *Bay City Blues*, a short-lived comedy-drama series about a minor league baseball team, the Bay City Bluebirds. Despite an impressive cast that also included then-relative unknowns Michael Nouri, Sharon Stone and Ken Olin, NBC aired only four of the eight episodes that were produced before cancelling the show for low ratings.

But that short-lived series made a lasting impact on Franz as there was also a baseball player extra on the series by the name of Joey Banks, who Franz came to learn is the son of Cubs' great Ernie Banks, Franz's boyhood hero. Through that chance connection Franz got to meet the Hall of Fame player he idolized as a kid.

"I got a nice personally-signed autograph from Ernie," Franz said, "and then I got to meet him several times. Throughout the years, we became sort of semi-friends. He was baseball for me."

Franz readily admits that for several years, he had not kept up closely with the Cubs. Then in 1998, he was invited to sing "Take Me Out to the Ballgame" at Wrigley Field during the seventh-inning stretch. Into the booth, he brought his three nephews, then between eight and 12 years old, to sing along with him. "That was an unforgettable experience and one that I will forever cherish," he said. "The opportunity that the Cubs organization gave me – and to bring my nephews with me – that was something that meant the world to them, because I come from a very, very, very Cubs family. They were introduced to the love of Cubs at birth. Their father is a die-hard Cubs fan as the rest of the family is, too. So that was the highlight of their life for them at that time."

The youngest of those three nephews, Cody Sharko, now works for the Cubs organization in its corporate partnerships division. "To know that this little squirt, who came into the box with me and sang 'Take Me Out to the Ballgame' is now working for the love of his life, the Chicago Cubs, and he was given this beautiful commemorative ring – it's just a story that goes full-circle and it's so wonderful to see…Through him I'm living vicariously."

For Franz, the Cubs' winning the World Series "was a validation of so many years of dreaming a dream and truly in your heart accepting the fact that that dream may never come true."

"It is something that I didn't expect to experience in my

lifetime," Franz said. "I thought there's no way that it was going to happen. It was something that I had loved all my life, and even though I didn't always follow them over the years, it wasn't that I had lost that love for them. It's just that life is long and there are many directions and many roads that it takes you. When you're young and you're playing baseball, that's the center of your world. You become older and all of that changes. But the love and the passion is still inside of you.

"Over all the years, I don't care where I am or who I'm with, if you asked me who do you like, I would always say 'I'm a Cubs fan. I always will be.' So when the dream came true, it was a validation. It was pretty wonderful."

9. Pat Hughes

Pat Hughes has been the golden "Voice of the Cubs" since his season-opening debut on April 1, 1996. He's become so synonymous with the franchise, Chicagoans may forget that the radio broadcaster's career spans an impressive 35 years, including twelve seasons with the Milwaukee Brewers. For two generations, Hughes has produced some of the most memorable and poignant radio commentary of the modern baseball era. Take for example, his iconic call of Mark McGwire's single-season, record-breaking 62nd home run in 1998:

"He drives one to deep left – this could be – it's a home run! Number 62 for Mark McGwire! A slice of history and a magical moment in St. Louis!"

The National League Central's long-running rivalry between the Chicago Cubs and St. Louis Cardinals is the stuff of legend. But Hughes' fundamental love of the sport, combined with his comprehension of a moment's weight, places his work at the top of the broadcasting profession – no matter which press box he's occupying.

Thankfully for fans everywhere, Hughes' mesmerizing voice and baseball expertise are interchangeable with the 21st century journey of Cubs Nation. And on November 3, 2016, he became the first Cubs broadcaster ever to announce that the team had finally, at long and painful last, won a

World Series championship:

"A little bouncer, slowly towards Bryant. He will glove it and throw to Rizzo – it's in time! And the Chicago Cubs win the World Series! The Cubs come pouring out of the dugout, jumping up and down like a bunch of delirious ten-year-olds. The Cubs have done it! The longest drought in the history of American sports is over, and the celebration begins!"

Six perfect sentences that brought a city, a state and many parts of the country to its feet. And for all his cool composure and professional experience, Hughes firmly grasped the "historical significance" of the occasion. "In 1908, the last time the Cubs won it all, there was no radio or television coverage," he said. "Throughout the 2016 playoffs, I was fully aware that if things progressed, I would be the first Cubs announcer ever to call a World Series win. I felt proud – and frightened."

Many diehard fans carried the memories and fervor of family and friends long gone that glorious November night. Like those pouring into the streets, Hughes understood that the moment was bigger than one voice. "It was emotional," he said. "I thought about the millions of Cubs fans that were waiting for this. I wanted to get it right – for them. When you're a live performer, you only get one shot. It was a five-hour final game with maximum pressure in every single way."

Hughes was raised in California as a San Francisco Giants fan. One of five kids born to a professor father, trips to the ballpark were a rare and revered treat. "We were not wealthy," he said, "and the drive was a 45-50-minute trip each way."

A young Hughes watched the 15 to 20 Giants games broadcast on television each season throughout the early 1960s. The remainder of his exposure was – fittingly – through the radio.

Though early loyalty belonged to the Giants, Hughes considered himself "a larger National League baseball fan. The National League of the 1960s was the golden decade of big league ball. Double-headers were common then. At one point in 1966, the Cubs and Giants were fielding nine future Hall of Famers combined, in a single day. Can you imagine that exciting level of play?"

One of those 1966 future Hall of Fame Cubbies was a young third baseman by the name of Ron Santo. Dubbing himself "single biggest Cubs fan of all time," Santo joined the WGN broadcast team in 1990, pairing with Hughes when the latter stepped up to the mike in 1996. Hughes grew up watching Santo "on the Game of Week" and given the opportunity to work with one of his idols, their on-air rapport quickly cemented. The Pat and Ron Show was born.

The duo collaborated until Santo's death in 2010. The partnership taught Hughes a great deal about the responsibility that would accompany him to a Cubs World Series. "A century without a win is a real burden," he said.

"Then it's 105, then 108 years and the weight grows heavier. I sensed that after every regular season loss with Santo. The disappointment was not just the day's fleeting emotion. It was a reminder of 108 years' worth of heartbreak."

Hughes has a unique perspective as a broadcaster who worked tirelessly through many "Lovable Loser" years, before suddenly and joyously representing World Series Champions. "It's a huge weight off of our collective shoulders," he said. "So many of us in the Cubs organization – on air, front office – we wondered 'When is this going to happen? Ever in our lifetimes?'"

And in the lifetime and career of Pat Hughes, "it" happened. Aware of the significance on the team, its fans and those who called decades of Cubs ballgames before him, Hughes is certain of his good fortune.

"Over a 22-year period, I've had as many great moments with this team as all other previous announcers combined," he said. "We were so pathetic for so long. From 1945 to 1984 – that's 39 years without a single postseason appearance. I've been given a gift. The 2017 season is my 35th. I no longer have to wonder if I'll ever broadcast a World Series game. I will never feel that emptiness at the end of my career."

The 2017 baseball season was a breath of fresh air for Pat Hughes. "That's the best thing about winning it all," he said. "Business as usual. It's just another baseball season. There's no longer that dread. We've won."

Hall of Fame players, broken curses and destiny notwithstanding, Hughes believes the Chicago Cubs owe it all to baseball's greatest fans. "Their support is unprecedented," he said. "It's genuine. It's impossible to quantify how much the fans influence everything – the atmosphere, the intimidating noise against the opposition. The greatest thing about being the 'Voice of the Cubs' for 22 years is the audience for which I get to perform. It's the best thing."

10. Stephanie Izard

Chef Stephanie Izard knows a thing or two about winning. The Chicago native and her impressive culinary talents first captured national attention in 2008. She appeared on the fourth season of Bravo's popular reality television competition, *Top Chef*. At the time, no woman had ever taken home the title. But after tasting was through, Izard emerged triumphant over James Beard nominee and fellow cuisine expert, Richard Blais.

Nine years later in 2017, Izard brought her knives over to the Food Network to compete in the *Iron Chef Gauntlet*. The Stamford, Connecticut-raised pro defeated the vaunted likes of chefs Bobby Flay, Michael Symon and Masaharu Morimoto. Once again, she'd been considered the underdog.

How does Izard view her own come-from-behind winning history, compared to the end of the Chicago Cubs' 108 years of Lovable Loserdom? Just as warm and satisfying, like a family gathering around the dinner table – rivalries, personal setbacks and all. "The Cubs have always brought people together," she said in an email exchange, "long before they won the World Series. Being a fan always meant loving them no matter what their record."

Although Izard's career journey has taken her many places, including residences in Michigan and Scottsdale, Arizona, where she graduated from the Scottsdale Culinary

Institute, the chef's heart never wandered far from her favorite baseball team. "I went to games with my family as a kid," she said. "But after culinary school, my friends took me to the bleachers for the first time. Such a profoundly exciting experience. Honestly, it's part of why I moved back to Chicago!"

For the past seven years, Izard and her partners from the BOKA Restaurant Group have owned and operated West Loop dining hotspot, Girl & the Goat. The runaway successful venture accelerated Izard's meteoric rise as a guru of grub. In time, the staple begat other venues such as the Little Goat Diner (across the street from Girl & the Goat), and Duck Duck Goat on Fulton Market. The omnipresence of the titular barnyard animal in Izard's restaurant nomenclature is more than a reflection of the chef's "nose-to-tail" cooking philosophy.

Members of Cubs Nation are quite familiar with the folklore. In 1945, Billy Goat Tavern owner William Sianis allegedly placed a lasting curse on the Chicago Cubs. According to the story, the odor emanating from Sianis' goat, Murphy, bothered other fans – so much that he (and his pet) were asked to leave Wrigley Field during Game 4 of the 1945 World Series against the Detroit Tigers. Incensed and offended, Sianis reportedly uttered the following words: "Them Cubs, they ain't gonna win no more." Whether Murphy's owner intended to stop the team from claiming another National League pennant, or a World Series title, has been a decades-long matter of intense debate.

What is certain is that the Cubs ultimately lost the 1945 Series, and went another 71 years without so much as a postseason appearance. Izard always believed the Cubs would be champions one day. That said, one of *Food & Wine Magazine's* "Best New Chefs" in 2010 was happy to do her part to counteract Sianis' bad juju. "My team of chefs and I got to cook on Wrigley Field a couple summers ago," she said. "We cooked goat in hopes of reversing the curse and we may have left a bone behind in the ivy. I admit nothing…but I think it worked!"

Whether it was cooked billy goat, the answered prayers of endlessly loyal fans or a winning combination of management and talent, 2016 was finally the Cubs year. When asked what the end of a century-plus of waiting means personally, Izard said, "I think it was the way the team won that made it so incredible. They always keep the fans on their toes!"

In times of victory and sorrow, the Chicago Cubs can't escape otherworldly elements. Jeff Santo, son of the late, great Cubs third baseman Ron Santo, described the conclusion of World Series Game 7 as "almost biblical." Indeed, the famous 17-minute rain delay that ultimately shifted momentum in the Windy City's favor could easily be interpreted as the hand of God. A little extra drama and tension before a satisfying outcome unites the fortunes of Stephanie Izard and the Chicago Cubs

The chef's life today incorporates the best parts of the Cubs winless past into the present and future. Her son, Ernie, born in 2016 and named "after Mr. Cub himself," is a tribute to Izard's all-time favorite player, Ernie Banks. She described the emotional joy of taking the baby to his first game: "It was me, Ernie and my dad – three generations of Cubs fans together for this experience." Before another game shortly following, Izard "was lucky enough to throw out the first pitch and Ernie got to stand on Wrigley Field. I'm so excited to show him that picture when he grows up to be a baseball player – or just a fan!"

The claim to "just" fandom reflects modesty that belies Izard's ongoing importance to the team – and the appetites of Friendly Confines visitors. As the 2017 season opened, the 2013 James Beard Award-winner for Best Chef Great Lakes achieved another first. She led a rotating roster of Chicago chefs featuring their cuisine at Wrigley. Other notable gourmets such as Rick Bayless and Graham Elliott comprised the All-Star kitchen club.

A popular item on Izard's ball park menu? Got the Goat tacos of course. Broken curses never tasted so delicious.

11. Sarah Jindra

Sarah Jindra, WGN-TV's Evening News reporter on transportation issues, traffic and breaking stories, was born on February 23, 1982. As a child growing up in suburban Westmont, Illinois, she believed her birth date made her part of an exclusive, heroic sports club. After all, 23 was the number worn by Michael Jordan during his magical tenure with the Chicago Bulls. Over on the South Side of Chicago, White Sox third baseman Robin Ventura wore the same digits. And future Hall of Famer Ryne "Ryno" Sandberg tore through Wrigley Field wearing number 23 for the Cubs. According to a young Jindra, so much talent wearing the same jersey was far from coincidence. "They all wore my number," she said. "How cool! Sandberg was always my favorite Cub as a kid. We were bonded by 23."

This early foray into numerology did not reflect a general, superstitious approach to the Lovable Losers. In fact, Jindra tended not to take the Cubs teams of the 1980s, 1990s and early 21st century very seriously – with good reason. "For me being a Cubs fan was always about having fun," she said. "They didn't win for so long, it was a joke. I never went to Wrigley Field expecting wins or for the Cubs to make headlines. I went to Wrigley because it was fun."

That's not to say the shift from perennial Major League Baseball also-rans to 2016 World Series Champions was unwelcome to Jindra. Quite the contrary. "Fast forward to 2015, and we start winning and the experience gets even better," she said. "Wrigley Field is such a great place to be. Baseball has always been in my family, been in our blood. But it never made or broke my ballpark experience when the Cubs struggled."

Particular concern for the trials and tribulations of the North Side team was nowhere to be found in Jindra's childhood home. Her father, a college ball player himself, was loyal to the White Sox – and a stickler for stats. "My dad has had season tickets to the White Sox for almost 40 years," she said. "We grew up with the team. My dad was a hard-core baseball fan. He always bought the scorecard and the little pencil. The hits, the runs, the strikeouts, everything was recorded by the book. It was all White Sox, all the time, until right after high school."

What changed after the newswoman graduated from twelfth grade? In another time-honored summer tradition, Jindra and her friends wanted to be where the boys were. And if they were at Wrigley Field, so much the better. "Some of the guys became peanut sellers," she said. "We went to watch them and not the game. But I started to think Wrigley was the neatest place."

Ultimately, one particular Cub fan caught Jindra's attention. And the rest, as they say, is history. "In college, I started dating my now-husband Brent, and he was a huge

Cubs fan," she said. "He's from Bloomingdale, Illinois and grew up watching and listening on WGN. In 2003, the Cubs got really good all of the sudden. We watched between classes at the University of Illinois at Urbana-Champaign because WGN was broadcast in town."

Few members of Cubs Nation ultimately regard the 2003 season as "fun," and Jindra is no different. "A lot of people dressed as Bartman for Halloween that year," she recalled. "To this day when I watch documentaries about the incident, I feel for the poor man. His life was changed. All of a sudden, winning – or not winning – was taken very seriously."

2003 remains a painful year for the Cubs legacy – a year when talent combined with hype and bad attitudes to create an implosion of hope. The ensuing heartbreak left a question in the minds of many fans. Would the proverbial "next year" ever find its way to the Friendly Confines? At least for Sarah Jindra, the fun resumed almost immediately with the 2004 season. "After college, we went to rooftop games," she said. "Unlimited food and drinks is the best thing ever in the mind of a recent graduate."

Post-graduate studies in New York eventually led Jindra back to Illinois, where she launched a career in radio and television news. Jindra's path ultimately took her to WGN, the superstation that created legions of Cub fans across 20th century America. It's in this capacity – hometown girl meets seasoned journalism pro – that she experienced the 2016

World Series Championship.

"I work at WGN, the station behind the Cubs for so long," she said. "It's such an honor. In November 2016, I had the opportunity to fly over the parade. I'd been to a Chicago Blackhawks Stanley Cup rally, which was cool in its own right. But flying over the Cubs parade – it was incredible.

"People were lined up on Addison, Lake Shore Drive, all the way down to Michigan Avenue. On the Magnificent Mile, the crowds were 8-10 people deep, stretching to Grant Park. It was amazing to see. It felt like the whole world showed up to celebrate with us. With literally a 48-hour planning window, fans came from everywhere. And everybody was mostly well-behaved. They cheered. They held hands. They cried. It was beautiful. I'll never forget it."

Jindra was not on duty during Game 7 of the World Series, but her family owns a real estate business in the Wrigleyville neighborhood. That fact provided a wonderful excuse to join the crowds before the emotional pandemonium – brought about by a victory 108 years in the making – was unleashed on Chicago. "We closed our business and showed the game on the wall," she said. "It was so great. When the Cubs were ahead, people started flooding Clark Street. Then they started to drop. Traffic slowed. We waited through the rain delay, the Cubs made a comeback and the people poured into the streets. It was just a good kind of crazy.

"People were overjoyed. There was no destruction. Some

of our reporters interviewed emotional people with pictures of long deceased relatives. A collective dropping of jaws. History had been made."

The Cubs won the World Series. The pressure is off and for Jindra, the good times at Wrigley Field are rolling along better than ever.

12. Len Kasper

Len Kasper didn't start out a Cubs fan.

"I grew up a Tigers fan," the Michigan native said during a telephone interview. "But I will never forget when we got cable in 1981 or '82 and WGN and TBS were on the package of main channels. WOR, I believe, in New York, too. So to be able to watch National League games – Cubs, Braves and Mets – was a really big deal to me.

"I was a Tigers fan at heart but I loved baseball in general, and I watched a lot of Cubs baseball when I came home from school in the early- to mid-'80s. It definitely had an impact on me."

Even back then, Kasper, who is entering his 14th season as the Cubs' play-by-play announcer, had a passion for calling games.

"I knew at a very young age that I wanted to be a broadcaster," Kasper said. "Ernie Harwell was my guy. He was the long-time Tigers radio voice, and I wanted to be him. I thought it would be the coolest job in the world."

Still, Kasper never imagined that he'd be sitting in the booth where broadcast legends like Jack Brickhouse and Harry Caray once were the voices of the team.

"It's still something that I don't know if it will ever fully sink in – just how huge this stage is," he said. "I've read and talked to a lot of people about the broadcast history of the

Chicago Cubs and WGN going back to 1948. Jack Brickhouse doing Cubs baseball from 1948 to '81. Harry's incredible run. Just so many great announcers who've been in that booth, and it has helped me, and I take that responsibility very seriously."

While Kasper tries to be his own voice, there is one tradition that he has carried over from the past, and that is Caray's signature "Cubs win!" call. He explained: "I got a nice letter from a lady – an older Cubs fan – at the end of my first year. She wrote me a very eloquent letter and said, 'When the Cubs win a game, you should say, 'Cubs win!' The way she explained it to me just made all the sense in the world. I thought, I'm not going to be here forever. Whoever sits in this booth, that is one thing that they should say. Pat says it on radio. I say it on television. I think it's a comforting thing for Cubs fans to hear, and it's kind of a neat thing to do to keep that thread going in terms of Cubs history."

Kasper admits that he has switched allegiances since being hired by the Cubs in 2005, after broadcasting stints covering the Green Bay Packers, Milwaukee Brewers and (then) Florida Marlins.

"I don't really follow the Tigers anymore," he said. "The Cubs are my team, and I am absolutely a fan."

While he is a fan, Kasper stresses that his job isn't to be the team cheerleader. "I do think, in terms of what I do in calling the game, there is a separation involved," he said. "I want the Cubs to win every day. I think that shows through in the call. But I also believe that there's a fairness and a credibility involved in calling the game for all fans.

"Mostly Cubs fans are watching – I understand that – but I believe my first and foremost job is to call the game, explain what's happening, describe the actions to the best of my ability, and make sure my partner Jim Deshaies has time to analyze and tell us why things are happening and how things are happening. Beyond that you just hope that the Cubs win as many games as possible. But I have to make sure that I treat my job with the respect it deserves, first and foremost, and let my personality shine through where it fits and it's appropriate."

From his perch in the broadcast booth, Kasper sees Cubs fans as "the best fans in sports – certainly baseball." He likens them to fans of the Green Bay Packers, a team he covered in his first broadcasting gig at WTMJ-AM in Milwaukee. "In the case of the Packers, the fans literally own the team," he said, "and the Cubs fans feel that way about their club. While it's a big market versus the smallest market in professional sports, it is kind of a family vibe sort of fandom. Where the Packers now have sort of surpassed the Cowboys as America's team in terms of the NFL, I think the Cubs have surpassed the Yankees in terms of baseball as America's team. WGN has a big impact on that.

"I just think it's the biggest fan base in the world, and we saw that last year when the team won the World Series and five million people came together in Downtown Chicago for the parade. People all over the world sending tweets and notes about how excited they were when this team won. We all anticipated that this would be the greatest moment of our lives, and it exceeded my expectations just in terms of the reaction. It solidified the fact that [the Cubs are] the most popular team in sports."

Harry Caray has a statue outside the entrance to the bleachers at Wrigley Field. Jack Brickhouse's signature "Hey Hey!" call is immortalized on the left field and right field foul polls at the iconic ballpark. But neither of the broadcasting legends ever got the chance to cover the Cubs in a World Series game. Kasper wasn't in the booth, but he was on the field broadcasting Game 7 of the World Series for 670 The Score just after they won, a moment that he said was "pretty surreal – a night I will definitely never forget."

The fan in him came out after that historic game. He rode in the victory parade in Chicago on a bus with his fellow broadcasters, attended a private party at the Metro music club and fireworks show at Wrigley Field, and took a selfie with Cubs' catcher David Ross and his wife Hyla.

For Kasper, the party hasn't stopped. "The celebration on a personal level continues to this day, to a large degree," he said. "But I would say the entire winter it was just a continuum of running into somebody who said, 'Wow that was amazing,' and 'I've been a Cubs fan my whole life and I never thought I'd see the day.' And just to see all the smiles on people's faces – that, to me, was so gratifying, just to see what that championship meant to so many people in Chicago and beyond."

13. Bill Kurtis

The first time television journalist, producer, narrator, and news anchor Bill Kurtis traveled past Wrigley Field, he didn't know what he was seeing. Nevertheless, the Friendly Confines made a big impression. "I was driving by the large structure at Addison and Clark and asked, 'What in the world is that?' Then," he said, "I figured it out. This was a temple dedicated to fun."

For nearly half a century, Kurtis has identified and analyzed a range of human experiences for American radio and television audiences. He's used to finding his way through cultural shifts. Born William Horton Kuretich in Pensacola, Florida, in 1940, fun was wherever the family traveled. The son of a U.S. Marine Corps brigadier general and decorated World War II veteran, young Bill quickly grew accustomed to life on the move. He also admired his father's service. A brief military career of his own brought him to the Chicago shores of Lake Michigan.

After a stint as an enlisted man in the United States Marine Corps Reserve, it was a commission as a Navy lieutenant that landed Kurtis in the Windy City. "I arrived in Chicago in 1966 and found an apartment for my wife and daughter on Fargo Street near the lake," he said. "For a long time, I thought there was only one baseball team in Chicago. The North Siders – the Cubs!"

Bill Kurtis' voice is singularly identifiable in a crowd. The phenomenon is a combination of natural gifts and early broadcast training. At age 16, he began working as an announcer for KIND, a radio station in Independence, Kansas. His family settled in the tiny town upon his father's retirement from the military, providing a semi-permanent environment for youthful experimentation.

However, the early radio experience didn't necessarily cement Kurtis' destiny. After a brief flirtation with law practice (he earned a juris doctor degree from Washburn University School of Law in 1966), and the aforementioned time spent in uniform, the man with the golden voice finally embarked on the broadcasting career that has made him a household name.

Kurtis' biography calls to mind another Chicago legend and almost-attorney – Cubs President of Baseball Operations, Theo Epstein. While working for the San Diego Padres organization in the late 1990s, Epstein studied at the University of San Diego School of Law – eventually earning his own juris doctor degree. Higher educational forays notwithstanding, Epstein's career path was singularly focused. Legend has it that the future Hall of Famer based class selections on attendance policy leniency – which accommodated long days with the Padres.

Also like Kurtis, a young Epstein dabbled in journalism, working as sports editor of the *Yale Daily News* during his undergraduate years. The experience eventually led to his first job in Major League Baseball as a public relations assistant with the Baltimore Orioles.

Though their paths ultimately forked, both Kurtis and Epstein enjoy a dramatic story. Say for example, the Sisyphean agony of the Cubs' 108-year World Series glory chase.

The narrative was sometimes plodding. "Gradually over the century," Kurtis said, "boredom with losing gave way to excuses that were half true, half myth. The fans knew they weren't true, but it took the edge off another year of losses. Delivered with a wink, we all knew what was meant." The noble suffering of the Chicago Cubs fan offered an easily accessible, emotional trope – the Lovable Losers and their steadfast loyalists. Hobbling curses, the inevitability of coming up short. The storylines wrote themselves over the years: Ron Santo and the heartbreak of 1969, the hapless Leon Durham's 1984 NLCS ball roll, the tears of 1989 and 2003.

Suddenly and satisfyingly, the narrative took an abrupt 2016 shift. "There came a year of youngsters who didn't know much about the decades of excuses," Kurtis said. "And they didn't care. Without the burden of carrying a century of baggage, they played as if their destiny was victory."

This time, curses mattered not. There were no spells, charms or talismans. Just consistent, solid, championship play. A triumphant combination of talent and faith. "To me, 2016 meant that endurance is better than luck," Kurtis said. "Focus is better than amazement. And winning is a lot better than a century of defeat. The Cubs are champs at last. It's Chicago. It's American."

A World Series on the North Side of Chicago as an act of patriotism is a beautiful idea. 2016 was not the first year that Wrigley Field evoked a sense of American pride and duty in Kurtis. An upbringing with military values is a lasting one. Kurtis waxed poetic about the day, one year after 9/11, when he was called to the field for a special assignment and how he was uplifted by the reverence of fans.

"The front office of the Cubs asked me to read a paragraph sent by President George W. Bush," Kurtis recalled. "The words were written to honor the first anniversary of [the terrorist attack]. Wrigley Field was packed. The summer afternoon was baseball hot. The announcer told the crowd that there would be a special ceremony. 'Please stand.'

"I walked past the teams lining the foul lines. The sports press waited at home plate. A single microphone stood there for me. I was struck by the silence, a stadium filled with 35,000 fans who seemed to be holding their breaths. The memory of 9/11 was fresh, and I felt the crowd was genuinely moved, anxious to show their respect.

"I read only a single paragraph, hardly a page. I held it with both hands as my voice echoed from stands to bleachers under the aged scoreboard. The crowd reacted as if I read the Declaration of Independence. With the final word, there was an explosion of sound, the best sound in the world, the sound of Cubs fans cheering."

Fourteen years later the crowds went wild again. It was a time of emotional release, a special instant of shared circumstance. Though tears flowed in the park, the streets and across the nation, they were not drops of sorrow. Rather, they were tears of pride over a mission long deferred and finally accomplished. The temple dedicated to fun shook with raucous, therapeutic joy.

Journalist Jonathan Alter and son
game 5 World Series

Actor Ike Barinholtz and wife Erica
Hanson in the Cubs' broadcast booth

CUBSESSIONS

WXRT rock DJ Lin Brehmer and son,
Wilson, at Wrigley Field

Brehmer sings "Take Me Out to the Ballgame" during
the 7th inning stretch at Wrigley Field

Pat Brickhouse with a photo of her husband,
Jack, the late, great Cubs' broadcaster

Dave Cihla and former Cubs shortstop Shawon Dunston
show off the "Shawon-O-Meter"

Dave Cihla raises the "Schwarb-O-Meter" after a Kyle Schwarber home run

Restauranteur Grant DePorter and former Cubs catcher David Ross at Harry Caray's Restaurant Navy Pier, January 2017

Comedian Tom Dreesen announces the Cubs-Dodgers
game wearing a replica 1908 Cubs uniform

Comedian Tom Dreesen as a batboy
at Wrigley Field

Actor Dennis Franz

The Cubs' broadcasters and the manager (left to right): Jim Deshaies, Pat Hughes, Joe Maddon, Len Kasper and Ron Coomer

Chef Stephanie Izard and her husband Gary Valentine with their first child, son Ernie, named after "Mr. Cub", Ernie Banks

Traffic reporter Sarah Jindra in the chopper

Cubs TV broadcaster Len Kasper interviews former
Cubs catcher David Ross

Broadcaster Bill Kurtis sings "Take Me Out to the
Ballgame" during the 7th inning stretch at Wrigley Field

A young Joe Mantegna rooting for his favorite team

Musicians Michael McDermott and Heather Horton
and their daughter Rain "Willie", at Wrigley Field

Beth Murphy at her Wrigleyville tavern, Murphy's Bleachers, with Pearl Jam frontman Eddie Vedder

Actor Bob Newhart and family celebrate the Cubs championship

Actor Nick Offerman and former Cubs pitcher Kerry Wood in the Cubs' broadcast booth (photo credit: Chicago Cubs Photographer Steve Green)

Mystery author Sara Paretsky joyous at Wrigley Field

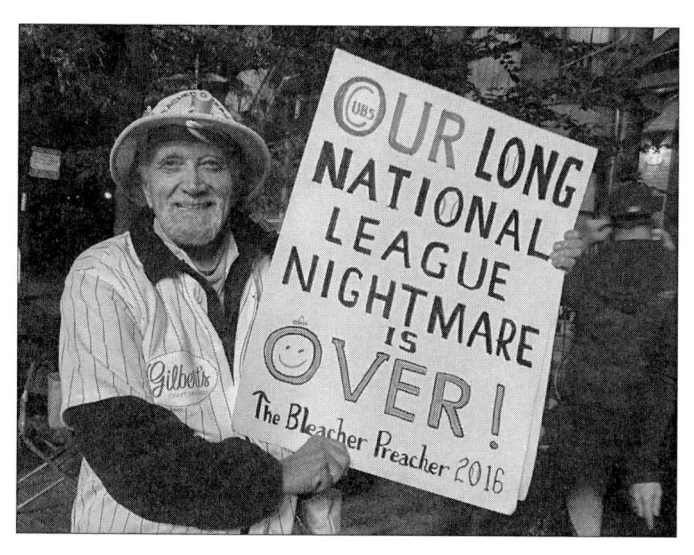

The "Bleacher Preacher" Jerry Pritikin (photo credit: Billy Cam)

Radio personality Jennifer Roberts and sister Becky Sarwate at Wrigley Field

Sam Sianis at his Billy Goat Tavern

Sam Sianis parades his pet billy goat around Wrigley Field, one of his many attempts to lift "The Curse of the Billy Goat"

NPR's Scott Simon in a classic pose with "Mr. Cub" Ernie Banks at Wrigley Field (photo credit: Peter Breslow)

Author and NPR host Scott Simon (photo credit: Marcos Galvany)

Chicago radio and TV broadcaster Bob Sirott
sports a Cubs uniform at Wrigley Field

Sirott in his vintage Cubs jersey

Legendary Chicago rock radio DJ Bobby Skafish wears the number of his all-time favorite Cub, pitcher Gregg Maddux

Michael Strautmanis, the Obama Foundation's vice president for civic engagement, at Wrigley Field

Former Cubs pitcher Steve Trout throws out the first pitch at Wrigley Field

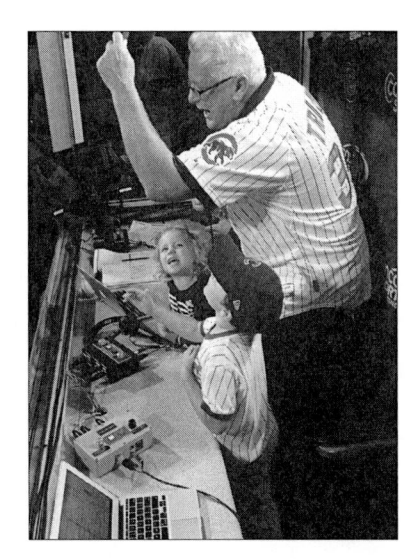

Trout belts out "Take Me Out to the Ballgame" at Wrigley Field

A young Scott Turow in his
Cubs uniform

Legal thriller authors Scott Turow and John Grisham at
Wrigley Field

Cubs' superfan Ronnie "Woo Woo" Wickers
and daughter Yolanda Linneman

Former Cubs ballgirl Kathy Wolter Mondelli
and her sister Lori Myers at Wrigley Field

Cubs ballgirl Kathy Wolter Mondelli

Actor Adrian Zmed and wife Lyssa Lynne

Brian Bernardoni wearing his World Series ring

Former Cubs' outfielder Jose Cardenal

Bob Dernier soaks it in atop a bus in the World Series celebration parade

Gene Hiser's 1974 Topps Baseball Card

Stewart McVicar's Cubs-themed man cave

Former Cubs' pitcher Rich Nye

The Santo family, Judy, Jeff, Ron, and Ron Jr.

14. Joe Mantegna

Sometimes, the tensions of a particularly close and important baseball game become unbearable. In these cases, a little solo quiet time may be necessary. That's the situation in which actor, producer, writer and director Joe Mantegna found himself in the late hours of November 2, 2016.

"It was such an emotional night," he recalled during a telephone conversation. "I didn't go to Game 7 of the World Series," he said. "I thought, 'If they lose, I'll be devastated – and in Cleveland.' So I was in L.A. at Taste Chicago, my wife's restaurant. To be shoulder-to-shoulder among all of these Cubs fans in the city was pretty awesome."

Then the longest 17-minute rain delay in Chicago Cubs history turned Mantegna into a hermit. "I watched the final inning from a Fox News truck in the parking lot," he said. "I couldn't stand to be around all those people if it didn't happen. So I'm staring intently at a 6 x 6-inch screen. With the final out, I started screaming in the truck and looked out at the door at the restaurant. It was dead quiet. It was like being in the middle of an otherworldly dream."

The news team barely had time to alert Mantegna to the 10-second delay in the live-game feed. And then he said, "The restaurant erupted. I realized I was one of the first people who wasn't physically at the game to see the Cubs win the World Series."

The star of CBS' *Criminal Minds* knows that fellow diehards relate to the need for community interspersed with quiet reflection. After all, Mantegna said, "We are a special society. That's what being a Cubs fan is all about. We come from all walks of life and experiences. I can talk Cubs with [journalist] George Will the same way I can talk to [musician] Eddie Vedder. Talk about two diverse people. This is a club of individuals who are passionate about the same thing."

Within the special society that comprises Cubs Nation, mini-tribes develop. Comedian Tom Dreesen and actor Adrian Zmed are two members of Mantegna's tribe – who also happened to be interviewed for this book. All three men are famous Chicagoland natives, but Mantegna does not regard the arc of his personal fandom as one defined by geography.

"I grew up around Garfield Park," he recalled. "And I was a Cubs fan before we moved to Cicero. On the West Side, to use another sports metaphor, baseball fandom was a jump ball. To the East you had Lake Michigan, and there were no teams playing in our neighborhood. It was our fathers and mothers who passed on their Cubs or White Sox loyalties. I was indoctrinated at a young age. I used to joke with my dad for years, asking, 'Why did you infect me with this disease?'"

On May 5, 2017, Mantegna threw out the first pitch at Wrigley Field for the 11th time. He and Dreesen maintain a friendly rivalry where this honor is concerned. "Tom and I are nearly tied in the category of people who've thrown out the first pitch most often," he said. Off the field, Mantegna explained his adult bonds with pals Dreesen, Zmed and other celebs in this way: "If I meet someone and they're a Cubs fan, it's like finding out you have the same birthday. You're immediately connected."

The club loyalist inspired a whole work about the unique relationships fostered by virtue of bleeding Cubbie blue. *Bleacher Bums*, the 1977 play written collaboratively by members of Chicago's Organic Theater Company, has been produced all over the world. A 1979 performance of the play was taped for PBS television, and in 2002 a made-for-TV movie adaptation was aired. Mantegna described the original concept as one driven by the twin theater concerns of storyline and economics.

"In my teens, I sat in the bleachers with my friends because it was cheaper than grandstand," he said. "I was also acting in plays during high school and junior college. During the early 1970s, I would go to the ballpark with friends and I started looking at the characters. I thought 'This is interesting.'

"35,000 people come here to watch a team that's most likely going to lose. But these diverse people show up every day to be frantic together. Then they go their separate ways and have nothing else in common. I thought, 'If I can capture this mania, what it is to be a Cubs fan, I think I'm onto something.'"

Convincing his fellow thespians to explore the idea was hardly a tough sell – since there was no money for anything else. "It was the end of the season and we operated on grants," he said. "[Chicago Organic Theater co-founder and director] Stuart Gordon gathered us together and asked what we could do on the cheap since we were out of money. I raised my hand."

The troupe spent some time at the ballpark taking notes and observing. The result, Mantegna said, was "The cheapest show you'll ever do. Just wear what you'd wear to a game as a costume. Take all of the seats out of one side of a theater, sit on bleachers and you don't need a stage. Anyone on a shoestring budget can mount this show."

The work's lasting popularity can be partly attributed to easy replication, but even in a post-2016 Cubs World Series reality, appetite for the production remains undiminished. "It's nostalgic," Mantegna said. "It took the team 108 years to get to last year. My mother just passed away in April at 101 years old. She was born in the middle of a seven-year losing streak. None of this happened overnight and there are many who will never forget the struggle and the love they carried for the team through it."

Whether or not the Chicago Cubs manage to put together a string of championships is almost immaterial for

Mantegna. "The Cubs are perfect proof that it's not easy to win a championship in the first place," he said. "But they have established themselves as contenders. We've played in three consecutive NLCS contests. We're in the category of guys you expect to contend and be there. It's an amazing change."

15. Michael McDermott

Follow the arc of Michael McDermott's musical career – and, by association, his personal life – and it's easy to see why his baseball allegiance gravitated to the Cubs, even though he was surrounded by Sox fans, having been born in Chicago's Beverly neighborhood and raised in Orland Park.

The funny thing is, McDermott didn't see it. Not until someone else pointed it out for him. "There was this one friend of mine who said, 'You're a Cubs fan, that explains a lot.' And I said, 'What does that mean?' And he said, 'You're the guy that people root for. It's very like you to be the lovable loser.'"

That's when it hit home. "Now, obviously, I could have taken great offense to what he said. But I realized, it's true – it's absolutely true. I was always the guy who didn't have great success but always had a lot of champions. There have always been people who are very passionate about what I do. But I never seem to make it to the dance. It's a narrative in my own professional life."

The parallels between his musical career and the successes and – more often – failures of his chosen team became evident. The history of the Cubs has of course been well-chronicled. There were the early back-to-back championships in 1907 and 1908 and then a lot of lean years thereafter.

For McDermott, who started performing in Chicago coffeehouses, bars and clubs in the early 1990s, incorporating elements of Irish music into an American folk rock sound, there was also early success. His 1991 single "A Wall I Must Climb," from the album *620 W. Surf*, reached No. 34 on the Billboard Mainstream Rock tracks chart. He was quickly touted as the next big thing by a number of publications. Comparisons were made to Bob Dylan and Bruce Springsteen. Horror novelist Stephen King became an early fan, even quoting lyrics to McDermott songs in two novels, *Insomnia* and *Rose Madder*.

All pretty heady stuff. And, as it turned out, all too much for McDermott, who found it hard to live up to the high expectations that had been placed on him in a fickle music industry. Like so many artists who taste early success, he fell into booze and drugs before finally finding his way back to a better place.

Read the bio on his website and you get a sense of where McDermott has gone and where he has landed today: "The missteps and failures that followed, the collapse of an industry that once embraced him as its next sensation, are troubles and travails that either ruin a person completely, or they force a change of attitude and staunch determination to gather one's resolve to not only survive, but overcome."

In other words, McDermott has faced his demons and lived to write more songs about it as he has done with his 2016 release *Willow Springs*, his 14th solo album. The autobiographical album reached No. 1 on Europe's Americana charts, making it McDermott's first album chart-topper in a musical career that has spanned over a quarter of a century.

For both McDermott and the Cubs, the trajectory has turned in a much more positive direction. Both have begun to embrace winning over losing.

"I remember at the time I was proud to be a Cubs fan because I was a very afflicted loser and I don't think like that anymore, and I don't think the Cubs do, either," McDermott said. "[The lovable loser] was an identity. To be a lovable loser is kind of a dangerous identity because it makes it okay to fail. For me, it made my failure okay. In retrospect, I don't think that was a great thing. Because it was an excuse.

"We all create our own narrative. Mine was the lovable loser. If only people understood me. If only people bought my record they would understand what a genius I am. That's all bullshit. The Cubs were a badge of honor, but it was an excuse for me not to be successful for a long time. Now I love that the narrative has been completely turned around and now there's expectation of great success, of sustained success, and I hope [the Cubs] have that.

"The Cubs were a template – a terrible, terrible template – and I based my life around them: I will be loved but I will always lose. That was my narrative. Now it's not. Victory is a narcotic as well. It's really the drug of choice."

His and the Cubs' stories are ones of resilience and perseverance – and, ultimately, hope. "The [Cubs] story is bigger than baseball," McDermott said. "It's a life story. The Cubs are an idea, an idea that regardless of your failure, you live to fight another day. It lends credence to hope in your life."

That all explains what being a Cubs fan has meant to McDermott. "I bleed Cubbie blue," said McDermott, who has sung the National Anthem at Wrigley Field several times now. "It's been a very long storied relationship that I've had with them, and it's been a great journey."

Now, like so many Cubs fans before him, he is passing on that relationship to Willie, the daughter he has with his musician wife, Heather Horton. "I'm glad my daughter's into it," he said. "I'm trying my best to have another generation of Cubs fans."

16. Beth Murphy

Talk about a room with a view. From her perch atop the bar she owns, Murphy's Bleachers, Beth Murphy gets a daily ringside look inside the beauty that is the Friendly Confines.

"Being a Cubs fan to me is a lot about the neighborhood," Murphy said as her eyes wandered across the street from her popular Wrigleyville tavern. "I enjoy sitting in my own bar looking up at the scoreboard. It's sort of amazing when I walk to work and there's a ballpark here."

At the corner of Sheffield and Waveland, the Bleachers' history traces back to the 1930s, when Ernie Pareti set up a hot dog cart there and served beer by the pail, naming it Ernie's Bleachers. In the early 1940s, Pareti erected a full-blown tavern on the spot. The bar became home to the legendary Bleacher Bums in the 1960s, when Ray Meyer took over it and renamed it Ray's Bleachers. Then in 1980, former Chicago police officer Jim Murphy bought it and gave it his surname. Just steps from the mouth of the entrance to Wrigley's bleachers, the bar became a nighttime hangout for several Cubs players, including Mark Grace, Rick Sutcliffe and Jody Davis.

Beth Murphy has continued to preside over the bar, after her husband lost his battle with liver cancer in 2003. "In the old days, the Cubs (players) came over here a lot," Murphy said, noting that the players don't frequent the local bars much in this day-and-age of smart phones and social media.

After the record-breaking championship parade, the players did come out as the party carried over to Murphy's Bleachers, where team president Theo Epstein and pitchers John Lackey, Travis Wood and Mike Montgomery gathered to celebrate with the fans, dance on the roof and sing "Go, Cubs, Go" and "We Are The Champions."

"I'm glad I wasn't there to see that," Murphy said with a smile. Though she missed the rooftop serenade, she was there when Epstein later returned wearing a "Billy Cub" costume, which had once been at the center of a lawsuit brought by the Cubs who had claimed it to be an unauthorized mascot.

The bar has also become a popular spot for A-list celebrity Cub fans. Actor Bill Murray, Pearl Jam's Eddie Vedder and The White Stripes' Jack White are among those who've partied on the Murphy's rooftop.

The problem with any room with a view is that the view can always be obstructed, and that's just what the Cubs did to the rooftop owners: when their battle with the rooftop owners got messy, they took away their view. Like any neighbor, the relationship Murphy has with the owners of the ballpark across the street is sometimes uncomfortable if not downright contentious. The two have butted heads on numerous occasions, most notably over the rooftops that surround the iconic ballpark on Sheffield and Waveland and their visual access inside the iconic ballpark. It was Murphy who took to battle on behalf of her fellow rooftop owners, leading the charge as the spokesperson for the Wrigleyville Rooftops Association.

"I think we've always had a little bit of a contentious relationship with ownership and maybe it just goes with the territory," said Murphy. "I think [the Cubs] should like us, but that's me."

The Ricketts family has slowly bought up most of the rooftops, using their deeper pockets to win the war.

But the long-running battle left Murphy, who grew up a Cubs fan in Albany Park, wounded in her relationship with the team. She acknowledged that the constant battles with the Ricketts family over their ballpark renovations and how they affect her business and other businesses in the neighborhood have taken a toll on her. "Yeah," she said, "it has affected how I feel about the Cubs a little."

When the Cubs won that dramatic Game 7 of the World Series and thousands took to the streets around the neighborhood to celebrate, Murphy said she "stood on the roof watching everything and just taking it in."

The view wasn't what she had always dreamt it would be. "I don't know if that game was very enjoyable for me, to tell you the truth," she said. "I don't remember that game being really that fun."

Murphy's greatest memories came in the days that

followed, especially the record-breaking championship parade. "The parade day was just amazing," she smiled. "They loaded the buses right outside the bar. We could see everybody. Our GM Freddy [Fagenholz] threw them Murphy's cups, so everybody on the bus had Murphy's cups."

But for her the most touching part of it was the spontaneous messages scribbled by fans on the brick wall of Wrigley Field below the right field bleachers. It was there that she paid tribute to her husband, who had given her that amazing view. "We brought a big, big ladder out there and wrote Jim's name as big and as tall and as high as we could," she said. "I felt that was just very moving and unexpected."

17. Bob Newhart

Legendary comedian and actor Bob Newhart has an idea about what first drew him to baseball, and Chicago Cubs fandom in particular.

"It's so important to have a live, engaged audience," he said. "I've been a Cubs fan since I was six years old. In the 1950s, the White Sox had [second baseman] Nellie Fox. He'd wait out the pitches and get on base. Then there would be a bunt and a fly ball and Fox would steal third. The Sox would win one or two to nothing. It was boring."

Over on the other side of town, Newhart said via telephone, suspense was always in plentiful supply. "You never knew with the Cubs. They were never out as long as [right fielder Bill] Nicholson was in the ballgame. The Cubs appealed to the showman in me."

One doesn't build and sustain a six-decade entertainment career without understanding an audience – without comprehending the special relationship between entertainer and loyal fans. Newhart likens the devoted, dispersed and diverse members of Cubs Nation to a live studio crowd, with a comparison from his own storied career. "On *Newhart* [1982-1990], I experienced how an audience can shape and change a show. The first time Larry, Darryl and Darryl came on, the crowd looks at these three guys. Deadpan they uttered the line they came to be known for: 'Hi. I'm Larry. This is my brother Darryl, and this is my other brother Darryl.' The audience went crazy. If we didn't have a live crowd, we never would have known about that reaction. Recordings take too long to get to air. You miss the moment. We had to have those actors back to *Newhart*. And they proved to be a staple. The movement of the entertainment industry away from the live audience is a great loss."

Newhart's anecdote calls to mind former Cubs outfielder Dexter Fowler's surprise return to the team in 2016, after a reported agreement with the Baltimore Orioles fell through. Fowler's "You go, we go" enthusiasm was a huge hit with teammates and Cubbie blue bleeders alike. And the player delivered the goods in a big way throughout the year's championship run. Fowler's belt-busting diving catch versus the Los Angeles Dodgers during the 2016 NLCS detonated an explosion from the stands.

Not even a defection to the St. Louis Cardinals for the 2017 season could turn the town against Fowler. Without his steady, good-natured playing, there is arguably no 2016 World Series Championship. Fowler enjoyed a hero's welcome upon his entrance to Wrigley in June 2017 for the season's first Cubs-Cardinals series. He collected his ring and a raucous round of applause from grateful fans – then hit a leadoff home run.

What would Dexter Fowler's fantastic turn in Chicago be without the thrill of an audience? Would we appreciate him as fully without witnessing the heroics firsthand?

That unquantifiable personal connection keeps fans like Newhart, and millions of others, returning to the Friendly Confines every season. This was true even during plentiful lean, winless years. Some of the dramatic pull came from sharing the emotional struggles of players like "Mr. Cub," [infielder] Ernie Banks. "I got to know Banks and his wife," Newhart said. "Marvelous human being – a nice man and just a great ballplayer. He suffered all those years with the Cubs and never even got to a playoff game. It was tragic."

But throughout every low moment, every reason for the fans to metaphorically exit through the turnstiles, Newhart reiterated, "You just never knew." He recounted a visit to Wrigley with his wife, Ginny, in the 1980s. "We went to the ballpark. Late in the game, the Cubs were down four to one. We thought we might try to beat the traffic on Addison. So we're walking outside to the car and suddenly we hear a tremendous roar. I asked someone, 'What happened?' and they said the Chicago pitcher hit a home run. Just like that, the team was back in it. You never give up."

The inability to give up on next year, the enduring bond between the team and its fans – these are dedications nearly impossible to shake. In Newhart's opinion, the long, emotional investment from all parties rendered the wee hours of November 3, 2016, a most exhilarating, if exhausting, reward. "I was so happy for all Chicago Cubs fans," he said.

"A World Series win after all this time was unbelievable. We had been so patient. The players had been so patient. The 2016 organization was very special.

"During the playoff run, I half-seriously sent a message to Max Berman, a PR guy with the Cubs. I asked him to please tell the team to give an 87-year-old man a break. Score more runs so I don't have to go through this agony every game. They sent me a 'W' flag, which was really nice. This group was confident."

That confidence, a break from the Lovable Losers resignation of the past, brought a championship trophy to Wrigley Field after an interminable 108-year wait. And according to Newhart, one of the oldest clubs in Major League Baseball is brand new again. "The Billy Goat is dead," he declared. "Now that we've won, the pressure is off. That's how I feel, and I hope it's the way the players feel."

Newhart shared a reborn perspective on loss. "When it happens," he said, "it's just the Cubs being the Cubs."

As the title of a memorable 1973 episode of *The Bob Newhart Show* [1972-1978] professed, "You Can't Win 'Em All." But even when we lose, said Newhart, "The crowd lets you know when the game is good. The live audience will stick with you."

18. Nick Offerman

For many children who grow up Cub, the promotional giveaways on certain home game days are nearly as exciting as the action on the field. In a March 31, 2016, post for *CBS Sports*, writer Matt Snyder compiled a list of the 30 best MLB ballpark promotions of the season. Number 14 on the list? The Ron Santo replica statue handed to incoming Wrigley fans before an April 30, 2016 home game.

Actor, voice actor, producer, writer, comedian and – yes – carpenter, Nick Offerman, fondly recalled youthful elation over particularly coveted freebies.

"As a teenager in the early 1980s, we'd take the whole family including aunts, uncles and cousins to Wrigley Field once a year, and we'd always do it on a giveaway day. My favorite was jersey day, and I think it was 1984 when the Keebler Elf graced the back of the three-quarter sleeve Cubs jersey. We wore those glorious shirts out until they were in tatters. It sounds pretty pedestrian nowadays, but we were not long on income in our household, so a free Cubs jersey was downright golden."

Offerman was born in Joliet, Illinois and grew up in Minooka, a town roughly 50 miles outside of Chicago. The son of a nurse mother and a junior high school social studies teaching father, intellectual curiosity was a hallmark of the home. The Offerman family may not have been wealthy, but they were rich in baseball enthusiasm and knowledge – especially as the qualities pertained to the Chicago Cubs.

"I came by [Cubs fandom] honestly," Offerman said. "WGN was our main family station for both radio and TV, so I didn't really have a choice. I have three siblings, and my dad was always a great resource of sports stats. So we would be quizzed on the Cubs' averages and career highlights as we trundled to and from our own baseball practices. Also in the 1970s and 1980s, there was no Internet and we didn't have cable. The Cubs games were by far our main household entertainment all through childhood."

From the analog days of the TV antennae in the living room to the digital era of highlights on demand, Offerman has dutifully admired and cheered the work of many legendary Cubs. However, the former star of NBC's acclaimed sitcom *Parks and Recreation,* confessed himself nearly stumped when asked which player of his youth received the honor of favorite.

"Ryne Sandberg springs to mind, as he was certainly the shiniest of the main protagonists back then. But our house also had soft spots for catcher Jody Davis, pitcher Rick Sutcliffe, Andre Dawson, Lee Smith and more. I think the players of that era stand out the most in my memory because once I left home for college and started adult life, the players seemed more distant. Really, though, watching Sandberg in the many years of his heyday was pretty amazing."

Sandberg announced his retirement in 1994, but that's not to say a young adult Offerman lost his passion for the Chicago Cubs or Wrigley Field. Rather, the ballpark experiences simply took a more hedonistic turn.

"I lived in Chicago during the mid-1990s, working in live theater," he recalled. "It was really hard to work baseball games into the intense schedule of eight shows per week, but when I could, it was usually a day game. My broke friends and I would sit in the bleachers and drink many beers, fending off their effect with hot dogs and peanuts while the Cubbies plied their trade. Looking back, the lack of responsibility that allowed us to indulge in day drinking and loud fan-hollering really takes on a halcyon glow that I have not enjoyed for a couple of subsequent decades. Ah, youth."

Offerman married fellow actress and comedienne Megan Mullally (NBC's *Will & Grace,* etc.) in 2003 – certainly an auspicious year for the suffering Cubs fan. And while the joys of day drinking may not be a feature of Offerman's life today, his early experiences resulted in a philosophical approach to Cubs fandom that still resonates in a long-awaited, post-World Series Championship world.

"It was character-building," he said of the protracted anticipation. "Rooting for the Cubs was great preparation for a life in which one must support and love a team – even though the team doesn't always win the final trophy. That's so very human when you think about it. Most of us provide laughs and triumphs as well as heartaches to our families and friends, so to have our humanity encapsulated by the plucky fellows at the Friendly Confines makes me want to be a better son, and brother, and husband, and neighbor – and beer customer."

And then one November, the solid, loyal citizen of Cubs Nation found the waiting at an end. In 2016, the home team won the final trophy after all. Offerman shared the disbelief, the joy and the gratitude of celebratory crowds pouring into the Chicago streets.

"We all kept saying it out loud over and over: 'The Cubs won the World Series.' Because for my lifetime – and my parents' lifetime before me – it was not a sentence that could be truthfully uttered. In life, sometimes your team wins all the marbles, and sometimes it falls short. But for longtime Cub fans, the payoff could not have been sweeter thanks to the many, many years of loyal and committed devotion."

A full bag of Cubs marbles sounds like a great promotional giveaway. Front office: you heard it here first.

19. Sara Paretsky

Sara Paretsky, recognized in 2011 as a Mystery Writers of America Grand Master, is best known as the author of the *V.I. Warshawski* novels. Featuring a smart and capable female protagonist, the works are a direct challenge to the 20th century dominance of male author/character pairings such as Raymond Chandler and Philip Marlowe, or Ian Fleming and James Bond. Adventurous, educated, multilingual, and a huge Cubs fan, Paretsky's "Vic" is not afraid of physical confrontations or getting dirty. The author and her heroine are rightly credited with transforming the role and image of women for the new millennium.

Her status as a literary revolutionary comes from a humble place – literally. Paretsky grew up in small-town Kansas at a time when gender equality – at least on the field – was as necessary as it was subversive. "I was educated in a two-room country school and girls played baseball as well as the boys," she said. "Being inclusive was the only way we could get nine people to field a team. I've been a fan of the sport my whole life."

Back then, Paretsky's home team was "the old Kansas City Athletics." The franchise played in the Paris of the Plains from 1955 to 1967. Kansas City Municipal Stadium offered the nearest venue for watching Major League Baseball. Within her immediate family however, cheering on the A's was a matter of geography, rather than legacy. The author's father "was from Brooklyn and a devoted Dodgers fan."

The boundaries of Paretsky's childhood baseball fandom were blurred by other factors as well. As a member of a religious minority in a very small part of the country, certain players inspired awe for their talent – and their very existence. "I was a Jewish girl in this tiny town, where we were practically the only Jews in town," she said. "Future Hall of Famer Sandy Koufax declining to pitch a World Series game on Yom Kippur? That was something."

It was during young adulthood that Paretsky's affinity for the Chicago Cubs began to take root. Like many rewarding stories, the author's journey to Cubs Nation began with baby steps. "It started in a funny way," she recalled. "I came from Kansas in 1966 to do community service to support the Civil Rights Movement. I was working for a church youth program. The White Sox wouldn't even take our phone calls, but the Cubs gave us free tickets. There were plenty of open seats at Wrigley Field at that time, so they could afford to be generous. I started to become a fan then, though not at an intense level."

The intensity that comes with bleeding Cubbie blue was cemented by two elements familiar to pre-1984 fans everywhere – copious day games and unexpected personal injury. "In 1977 I want to say, I sprained my ankle rather badly and had to take off work for a couple days," she recalled. "The

Cubs were the only thing you could watch on daytime TV then that wasn't mind-numbing. Bill Buckner was playing first base. The man had doggedness and played through his pain. He soaked his ankles in bags of hot salt before every game to stay flexible. He was a model for me in my injured state, and kind of my model for life. Not only must we play through the pain in a literal way, but generally, you keep going and do what you have to. Because what else is there? Buckner was not the greatest player, but he was inspiring."

By 1984, Paretsky had long returned to the field, so to speak. And the Cubbies were looking at their first postseason appearance since 1945, a National League Championship Series against the San Diego Padres. At the time, the author was toiling in a downtown Chicago insurance office and the personal electronics industry was taking off. "All over town they were bringing out two-square-inch TVs," she recalled. "People were hiding them in their desk drawers. Not a lot of work got done. I'll tell you that much."

From the exciting electricity of potential to the agony of defeat, the city's mood shifted rapidly. Paretsky got a taste of the emotional highs and lows that historically accompany Cubs fandom. "When they lost that third game and Leon Durham let the ball roll by I thought, 'Oh God,'" she said. "I went into such a depression. It was like my best friend had died. It went on for a long time, something like a month, and then I said, 'I can't let this team hold me hostage anymore.'"

Paretsky was resolute in this opinion…until 2003 of course. The Lovable Losers had one more tragedy in store for the mystery author. "I was on a book tour and of course the Cubs were playing the Marlins," she reflected. "I was doing an event in Lawrence, Kansas, my home town. The Cubs went ahead during Game 6 and I thought, 'This is it! We're in the World Series!' I got back into the car just after the Bartman moment, and I knew then that we were doomed. It wasn't in them to recover and get through that last game."

From the vantage point of 50 years of frustrated Cubbie hopes and dreams, what does the 2016 World Series Championship mean to Paretsky? Her experience as a writer of suspense permitted nurturing an against-all-logic intuition that ran throughout the team's historic season. And the story finally has an end of sorts.

"I felt it all year long," she confessed. "Something is going to happen. After the impossible finally became reality, a lot of friends I have in the Boston area said, 'One World Series isn't enough.' Well one is enough for me. Losing streaks don't get me the way they used to.

"My husband and I had a World Series party for Game 1, and that was such an unpleasant shocker, we decided to watch privately from then on. Then Game 7. I didn't think they were coming back until the rain delay, but then I felt a karma shift. I was suddenly pretty sure they were going to win it all, though my Jewish, eastern immigrant upbringing warned me not to tempt the 'evil eye.'"

There was nothing evil about Anthony's Rizzo's ball-pocketing final play to announce it definitively. The Chicago Cubs were World Series Champs – at last. The new world order set Sara Paretsky free to be flip about the impact of the long wait on her craft. "Being a fan makes me a greater writer," she said, "because great art is built upon suffering."

> "When the *V.I. Warshawski* movie was being filmed, the studio rented Wrigley Field for the night. The extras were in the stands and waiting, so I did a bit of hot dogging and ran the bases. The crowd cheered me on, the lights at full power. As I finished my run, I fell onto home plate. I tell you it was one of the biggest moments of my life. That grass was everything I imagined and even more. It was like velvet."
>
> — Sara Paretsky

20. Jerry Pritikin

Jerry Pritikin, a Chicago native and Cubs cultural touchstone, remembers the feeling of promise after a long stretch without a World Series win. In this case, however, the year was 1945. It had been 37 seasons since the Cubs won it all, and this is where the story of the Bleacher Preacher begins.

"I was eight years old," he said. "I went to some games with my dad and he sat in the gambling section – right center below the scoreboard. We knew an old family friend who'd lost an apartment building there. My dad was not a gambler by any means, but he used to sit in that section.

"That year the Cubs clinched the National League Pennant. There were only eight teams in each league, so if you won, you went to the World Series. I asked my dad to take me to the Series, but he thought I was too young. He made me a promise though, 'I'll take you next time.'"

Pritikin and his father never had the chance to attend a World Series baseball game together, but the elder, known as "the Tomato King of the South Water Market," made sure his son was prepared for lifelong citizenship in Cubs Nation.

"He got up at 2 a.m., Monday through Friday to go to work," Pritikin said. "But he made sure to give me a crash course in Baseball 101. He learned in the old, second West Side Park [1893-1915]. My dad picked up pop and beer bottles to get free passes. Or else he snuck in. With my brother and me from 1945 and up, the official language at our table was baseball."

The son of Jewish parents who emigrated from Russia, the elder Pritikin prized baseball as a game synonymous with America. Like so many kids born into immigrant families in the first half of the 20th century, baseball offered an exciting forum for bringing cultures together.

"There was one major Jewish ball player when I became Cubs aware – Hank Greenberg," he said. "I received a crash-course lesson on him from my dad as well.

"On April 17, 1947, the Cubs played the Pittsburgh Pirates and Hank Greenberg had just been sent to the Pirates. He was the first hundred-thousand-dollar ball player. My dad took me, my brother and two friends to the game. Opening Day tickets and we sat in box seats. It was such a treat."

Pritikin tells the story like it was just yesterday. "It was a 0-0 game into the sixth inning," he said. "Then Greenberg hit a double, driving in the game's only run. I didn't know whether to clap or cry. The Cubs started the season losing one to nothing. For me, this was an instance of heavy, complicated feelings toward being a Cubs fan."

A month after that Opening Day game in 1947, full of mixed feelings, Jerry Pritikin had a seat to watch another kind of cultural history unfold. "My brother and I were in the ballpark when Jackie Robinson made his debut. We had to get off the streetcar four blocks before Wrigley because there was such a large crowd. There were 47,000 or so people at the game. No fire laws back then. People sat in the aisles and on the fences.

"The thing I came away with was this – the only time I heard booing was for Dixie Walker, a right fielder for the Brooklyn Dodgers. Jackie was a big deal right away.

"There were a great many black people at the park, dressed for Easter Sunday at church. My brother and I sat in front of a good-looking black couple. Twenty to 30 percent of people brought binoculars with them that day. I've never seen anything like that before or since. The black gentleman my brother and I sat near had some high-end binoculars and he let us look through them. Jackie never got on base that day and he made an error, so his debut in Chicago was not that great. The whole canvas changed after he arrived though.

"Jackie brought the high-level base stealing. He made pitchers nuts and brought excitement that was needed. And of course, he opened the door. I had seats to watch new black players come in over the next few years."

For all of the early, exciting seasons young Jerry Pritikin beheld, the man who became known as "the Bleacher Preacher" in the 1980s for his semi-serious attempts to convert the fans of opposing teams has found a gifted memory tough going. Take the entire 1950s for example.

"The teams were cellar dwellers," he recalled. "They often

just closed the upper decks at Wrigley Field during games because no one was there. Baseball was such a different sport. Several owners went to jail for trying to hoard cash. There were no TV deals. The Cubs, Cardinals and New York teams sold rights to small cities for ticker-tape reads of their games. Just listening to those Cubs teams was rough."

It seems appropriate that the Bleacher Preacher showed faith and loyalty through the many lean years of Cubs competition. But even as the team began to show signs of new life in the 1980s, Pritikin wasn't necessarily a fan of the impact on Wrigley Field.

"To me, the lights were the beginning of the end," he said. "Wrigley started becoming like any other park. In 1991, I was in an article. They raised bleacher tickets from four to six dollars and I boycotted them. I haven't been to many games lately because I feel guilty spending what they charge today for an experience I'm used to."

The wistfulness of the boy who used to clean Wrigley Field in exchange for free tickets shows in his reaction to the 2016 World Series Championship. Now approaching his 80s, the Bleacher Preacher has experienced adult disappointments more profound than a few decades of bad baseball.

"I never really celebrated the World Series because I was so devastated by Hillary Clinton's loss to Donald Trump in the 2016 presidential election," he said. "That doesn't mean I didn't care, because of course I did. But now I'm worried for all of us in this country."

> "In 1981, when I lived in San Francisco, I was involved with a local production of the play Bleacher Bums, handling publicity. The show was scheduled for a six-week run but lasted over a year and a half. I turned the lobby of the theater into Wrigleyville West and became known as the Bay Area's resident Cubs fan. It was there, and not in Chicago that 'the Bleacher Preacher' came into being."
>
> — Jerry Pritikin

21. Jennifer Roberts

Jennifer Roberts, one half of "Koz and Jen," the weekday afternoon team on Chicago FM radio's 101.9 The Mix, never deliberately considered her status as a diehard Cub fan. "I inherited a legacy," she said. "My Cubs fandom was decided before I was born. It wasn't a choice. It was just something I grew up knowing. If you were part of the family, you were a Cubs fan."

Roberts took her cues from a special mentor. "No one was more Cubs loyal than my beloved Grandma June," she said. "The team was her everything… well, the Cubs and White Castle sliders were, anyway. She worked hard all of her life to support six kids as a waitress.

"She passed away in the summer of 1991, and each time, before or after that the Cubs gave fans reasons to hope, I found myself wanting it so damn bad – for her as much as myself. I wanted to witness a Cubs World Series win, so she could be satisfied from above, knowing her kids and grandkids got to experience what she didn't live to see. The only thing she loved more than the Cubs was her family."

Raised in the North Center neighborhood of Chicago, just a short walk from Wrigley Field, Roberts and her immediate family (full disclosure: Jennifer Roberts' only sibling Becky Sarwate is a co-author of this book) made attending home games a favorite summer ritual. Both of her parents grew up and married in the area, and grandparents on both sides swore allegiance to Cubs Nation. This endowment lends itself to playful humor when Roberts is asked about certain physical traits.

"I'm very fair skinned," she said. "Not 'pale,' because that implies illness and I'm doing just fine. But because of my complexion, it's very easy to see my veins. One runs prominently under my right eye. People always mistake it for a blue pen mark, and my long-running response is 'Oh no, that's just the Cubbie blue running through.' Then I proceed to show them other transparent signs of devotion along my arms (I keep my legs covered)."

Roberts' family lineage, indeed the very veins on her face are aligned with the Chicago Cubs and their history as Lovable Losers. While both of these realities instill her with a strong sense of pride, there have been times when viewing herself as synonymous with the North Side baseball team has been, shall we say…less rewarding.

"October 14, 2003 is a date I and many Cubs fans will never forget. I speak of course of the horrid 'Steve Bartman incident.' I was there and yet I wasn't. Fully expecting the Cubs to win a trip to the World Series for the first time since 1945, I was restaurant/pub hopping in Wrigleyville with my friend Gary. It was clinching night and though we were too late and poor to buy game tickets, we felt we needed to be in the atmosphere, if not the Friendly Confines."

"Oh Lord, was that a bad day," she said, gripping the armrests of her chair as though the memory is every bit as painful as 14 years later. "When Game 6 of the National League Championship Series ended, there was so much disappointment and anger. We were all looking for someone to blame. Many chose Bartman, but within our circle of family and friends, Gary and I took some heat. We became known as jinxes."

Another trait that Jennifer Roberts inherited from her diehard Cubs fans family, and a variable that connects her to worldwide citizens of Cubs Nation, is a superstitious nature. She took the 2003 jinx allegations seriously and has not ventured near Wrigley Field during a playoff run since.

"I accepted the blame," she said. "I vowed to stay away in 2015 when the Cubs made it to the postseason, and of course in 2016 when they had the best chance in years to win it all. I watched every playoff game from the safety of my office or living room. And of course, the Cubbies ultimately won the World Series, so you're welcome, Chicago."

These days the married mother of two experiences split baseball loyalties in her home – a testament to the tolerance, as well as team fidelity, imparted to her as a young Cubs fan. When you grow up taunted by accusations that your club is little more than the world's greatest tourist attraction, you learn to keep the trash talk to yourself.

"My husband is a White Sox fan," she said. "So when they

won the World Series in 2005, I was supportive and into it. At the end of the day, when the Cubs are out, I'm a Chicago girl. He's not usually great at returning the favor, but he went all in with me in 2016 – watching all the games, wearing a Cubs shirt for the first time in his life, praying (literally) that the Cubs would do this for his 'love.' It was great to be on the same side."

Jennifer Roberts was home in the suburbs for Game 7, which she labeled "an *insane* experience that will forever live in the history books and in the hearts of fans old and young." The shifts in momentum, the intervals of hope and dread, the rain delay that felt interminable. The experienced broadcast professional of more than a decade was reduced to the emotional rubble of Jane Q. Fan.

"The final out…oh my God. I just crumbled. I was a mess of tears and feelings of relief, excitement and shock. It was a lot to take in. The years of suffering had ended in victory. I just cried unabashedly in front of family and in-laws, who were wise not to judge or make fun.

"Then FaceTime lit up on my iPhone and it was my older sister and former accuser, the only other person who truly understood what I was feeling. We wished we were together, dropped a few excited F-bombs, said, 'I love you,' and went back to our separate celebrations."

As it was for many jubilant fans that November night, sleep was tough to come by. "I stayed up until 3 a.m. watching coverage," she said. "Long after everyone else had gone home or to bed. I finally closed my eyes as night turned to day."

And just as her grandmother would have done with her own children, given the opportunity, Roberts and her youngest daughter celebrated the next day together. "After I rose from the most blissful slumber in years," she said, "my kid and I went shopping for merchandise. She didn't take one sick day all school year, but she took a Cubs day. I'm raising her right."

22. Sam Sianis

A billy goat walks into a World Series game…

It sounds like the set-up for a joke. And perhaps that's all it ever really was – a joke played on a weary fan base, spun by tellers of tall tales over glasses of whiskey and rye, which grew with time into arguably baseball's all-time greatest urban legend: The Curse of the Billy Goat.

"It's all true," insists Sam Sianis.

If anyone would know, it would be him. It was his uncle, William "Billy" Sianis, a Greek immigrant and owner of the Billy Goat Tavern, who brought his pet goat, Murphy, to Wrigley Field on October 6, 1945, during Game 4 of the World Series.

"My uncle found a baby goat outside his bar," Sianis said. "He adopted it. Gave it a bottle of milk. He would take that goat everywhere. It was his mascot. Well, okay…one day, he decided to take the goat to Wrigley Field. It was the World Series in 1945. My uncle bought two tickets for $7.20. One ticket for himself, one for the goat. They wouldn't let the goat in."

An usher called team owner Philip K. Wrigley. "Mr. Wrigley would only let my uncle in, not the goat. [Wrigley] said, 'The goat smells.'

"My uncle left the ballpark, went back to his tavern. When the Cubs lost the World Series, my uncle sent a telegram to

Mr. Wrigley. It said, 'Who smells now?'"

The accounts of what actually took place from that point forward in the story are as hazy as a smoky tavern. And perhaps that is because the true origin of the curse story likely began not at that World Series game, but instead, years later, in Sianis' bar, a popular watering hole for Chicago's hard-boiled newspapermen.

"My uncle was what you'd call a great promoter," Sianis acknowledged. "He told everyone about the goat. And he told everyone about the curse he put on the team. It took on a life of its own."

When his uncle died in 1970, Sianis inherited the subterranean tavern on Lower North Michigan Avenue, which kept gaining fame through frequent mentions in the newspaper columns of Mike Royko and the Olympic Café *Saturday Night Live* skit that was based on the Billy Goat.

Meanwhile, as the Cubs kept losing, the legend of the curse only kept growing – despite Sianis' many attempts to break it.

"I tried to break the curse several times," he said. "I brought a goat named Socrates to the ballpark, but they wouldn't let me in. That was in 1973. I even said, 'All is forgiven,' but they still wouldn't let the goat in.

"On Opening Day in 1984, they finally let me in with the goat. We walked across the grass in Wrigley. The team had a great year. They almost made it to the World Series. Just one game away. But the curse was strong … strong because my uncle had such a strong personality."

Ten years later, in 1994, after the Cubs' worst start in team history, Sianis again brought his goat to Wrigley Field, in an effort to end a 12-game losing streak. Initially, he was denied entry but when a crowd started a chant of "Let the Goat in!" Hall of Famer Ernie Banks stepped in and escorted Sianis and his goat into Wrigley. The Cubs won the game, ending the streak, but it wasn't enough to rescue another losing season.

Then in 1996, Sianis was back with his goat, this time on the stage of *The Tonight Show* with Jay Leno, along with Cubs' first baseman Mark Grace, in yet another attempt to lift the curse.

Whether you believe the Curse of the Billy Goat to be true or nothing more than a fictional creation of some mischievous newsmen and a family of savvy Greek showmen, it reached almost mythic proportions, being told in popular literature – including John Grisham's *Calico Joe* and *The Litigators* – and in song by baseball folksinger Chuck Brodsky.

And it kept on growing until 2016, when the Cubs finally cast aside the curse that Sianis' uncle had placed on the team 71 years earlier.

"One of my sons said there was a lot of magic in the 2016 season," Sianis said. "He sure was right about that. The magic of that great season ended the curse. It's officially over now."

Sianis watched the epic Game 7 in the place he is most comfortable, the Billy Goat, which was packed with family and friends. "We brought a goat in, too," he said. "Another curse killer."

"If I close my eyes, I see that last out over and over again, like a dream. I was so happy … happy for all the diehard Cub fans, happy for Chicago.

"I thought of my dear friend, Mike Royko. He was the first person who came to mind when the game ended. I thought of how much he truly loved the Cubs, even when he got mad and complained about them being horrible at everything.

"But it happened. It finally happened! And nothing, not even another goat, can take that away from Chicago.

The Cubs' story of overcoming so many obstacles to finally succeed is one to which Sianis can easily relate.

"It's the American Dream," he said. "The American Dream I've lived, too. If you work hard and do the right things, you'll be okay in the end.

"It's also a family affair. Chicago is so much a part of my extended family. When the Cubs win, we win … the whole city wins."

As for his own place in Cubs' history, Sianis said he would like to be remembered as "Someone who had a heart. Someone who wanted to make people happy. Someone who loved Chicago.

"The Cubs and the city are … how do you say it? Intertwined. They're together through thick and thin. I see it every day. It's not always easy, but that's just the way it is in the world."

Said Sianis: "I love the Cubs. I love them because they are Chicago. And Chicago means everything to me. Loving the Cubs means believing … believing in both the good and the bad things that happen but believing all the time."

23. Scott Simon

Scott Simon, the host of NPR's *Weekend Edition*, has a deep and unusual connection to the Chicago Cubs. Charlie Grimm, who played first base for the Cubs and managed them in the World Series in 1945, was his uncle. Jack Brickhouse, the former Cubs broadcaster whose signature "Hey! Hey!" call marks the outfield foul poles at Wrigley Field, was his godfather.

For a boy who grew up on Chicago's North Side, the son of comedian Ernie Simon and actress Patricia Lyon, those familial ties served as a golden ticket to the Friendly Confines.

"My father and I, almost every weekend the Cubs were in town, would go to Wrigley Field and we would go immediately to Uncle Jack who would bring us down on the field," Simon said during an interview after a book signing in Skokie for his latest memoir, *My Cubs: A Love Story*. "It made an impression on me this way, meeting all the people I did – Ernie Banks, Gene Baker, Stan Musial. It permanently affected the way that I see athletes. I know athletes can be pricks, and often are. They're tough and competitive and fiery. But all of that being said, the best of them in all ways remember what it was like to be a kid and idolize athletes. And I found that the best of them are really touched by the way kids feel about them and go out of their way to be nice to them. And that really affects me. As a father now, I think that's absolutely wonderful. I think part of the reason they become an athlete is to see that kind of look in a kid's eye that they once had for someone else."

Those childhood experiences grew into the lifelong love affair he's had with baseball in general and the Cubs in particular.

"The Cubs have been a love I have shared with my father and my grandfather, my wife and my daughters, and sometimes a language to connect us when words might only drive us apart," Simon writes touchingly in *My Cubs*.

He explained the idea for the memoir: "I became comfortable with the idea of a love story because I like to think, particularly now that the Cubs have actually won their first World Series in a hundred and eight years, love is something that can deepen with time. It can mature. It can change contours. It can be of a different texture and a different tone. And I think that's probably what's going to happen now."

The lesson that loving the Cubs teaches, he professes, is that "life is more about trying than winning…and trying again, and then again."

To be a true Cubs fan, Simon argues, one must understand the team's history. In *My Cubs*, Simon gives a primer that is blended with his personal thoughts and impressions on topics familiar to any long-time fan. He blames the team's historic losing streak not on curses – like the so-called Billy Goat Curse that originated from that 1945 Series his uncle managed – but on inept management that was slow in breaking the color barrier and a focus more on a ballpark than on the team that played in it.

"It's not like being a fan of any other team," he said. "It's not like any other fan experience that I know of in this country. Maybe Boston comes a little bit close. But the characters, the history, the tradition, the mortification, the embarrassment, the living legend that we have had right in front of us that demonstrates that the important thing isn't to win but to try and then keep on trying…and when that doesn't work to try something else but to keep on trying. To me, that is life. To me, that is one of the best things that I can impart to our children."

To Simon, there can be no fair-weather Cubs fan. "You can't turn on the TV once every five years and be a Cubs fan," he said. "You are not a Cubs fan until you know what it's like to have your heart torn out of your body and eaten by a goat. That's being a Cubs fan."

The 65-year-old writer and broadcaster wants the two daughters, Elise and Lina, that he and his wife, Caroline Richard, adopted from China to have a full understanding and appreciation of just what it means to be a Cubs fan.

"Being a Cubs fan to me is recognizing the history of not winning for 108 years. Not only not winning but losing in improbable and comic ways – ways that probably should make professionals chagrined and embarrassed about what happened. But accepting that history and the character-building that goes along with it. And, you know, to a degree, embracing it. It made the Cubs distinctive. I think it was long past the time to give it up, but I think it also made the Cubs distinctive. I'm glad that our daughters now know a winning vintage of Cubs. But at the same time, I want them to know the history. Because I think that's an important part of what it is to be a Cubs fan. I think it's an important part of what it is to be a North Side Chicagoan. I don't want them to have this dark star in their life. But I want them to know what this represents."

That moment the Cubs ended their 108-year World Series drought he recounted in vivid detail as if it still runs on an endless loop in his head.

"I was sitting on the sofa with my wife, well, no, how can I say I was sitting on the sofa…I was not sitting on the sofa with my wife. I was standing up in anxiety. My wife and I were both standing up in anxiety and holding onto each other's hands and on that last play I sort of dropped my hands, although I kept hold of hers. Kris Bryant's leg is slipping, and I can see from the moment it left his hand…I thought it was, well, you know… I thought it was going to go sailing over Rizzo's glove… and, as my wife described it for me, I looked like I had just seen a spaceship land. She had just never seen a look like that in my eyes… and that was quickly accompanied by tears. I began to cry, and she began to cry. I couldn't believe it.

"And then I did sit down. My wife, who is French, doesn't believe in saving Champagne for special occasions. She thinks Champagne should be more in the routine order of things. Someone on the Cubs had sent us a bottle of wine with a 'W' on it. We had drunk a fair amount of wine just to get through the game. She said we should open that and I said, 'Well, we've both had a lot to drink.' And then we both said, 'Oh, come on!' And we opened that, and we watched all of the postgame interviews and all of that.

"My wife eventually did go to bed about a half hour before me, and I just sat there in the relative quiet of darkness and just thought, 'I can't believe it.'"

24. Bob Sirott

As a young Cubs fan Bob Sirott tucked a transistor radio underneath his pillow at night. He'd tune it to WGN radio and fall asleep listening to Jack Quinlan and then Jack Brickhouse.

"I think that's how I got the radio bug," said Sirott, who went on to become one of the top radio disc jockeys at WLS from 1973 to 1980 before moving to TV for many years and then landing back on the radio, including a stint in 2017 on WLS, the station where he first rose to fame.

Quinlan, whose broadcast partner was Hall of Famer Lou "Good Kid" Boudreau, hooked him at that early age. "I loved him as a kid, and when I heard tapes of him when I got older I realized how great he was," Sirott said in a telephone interview. "He was a great reporter and had a great voice and a real sense of humor and a spirit of fun. I think even more so than Jack Brickhouse, Quinlan got me into [radio]. I was shattered when he was killed in a car crash in 1965."

In the many broadcasting hats he has worn over more than four decades, Sirott has met and become friends with many of his childhood baseball heroes. This included the biggest stars like Ron Santo and Ernie Banks to lesser ones like Bill Bonham and George Mitterwald. "Whenever I was around those guys," he said, "I would turn back into that 10-year-old kid."

One experience particularly stuck with him. Now and then, he'd hang out during batting practice before heading downtown for his afternoon shift at WLS. "Ernie Banks was on the field and I'm walking off and he asks me where I'm going. I tell him I'm going to work, and he says, 'Can I hitch a ride with you?' and I'm thinking, 'Are you kidding me?'"

As Sirott tells the story, Banks hopped in with him in his little red MG sports car and as they're driving south on Clark Street, just a few blocks from the ballpark, they come to a red light. "I notice this guy in his backyard mowing his lawn. So I'm making small talk and I say, 'Hey Ernie, shouldn't that guy be going to the game today instead of mowing his lawn?' And Ernie says, 'You know, you're right,' and he jumps out of the car and runs over to this guy who's mowing his lawn and puts his arm around him. I don't know exactly what he's telling him, but I imagine he was telling him that he should go to the ballgame. When he got back in the car, I looked down the passageway and I see this guy and he's standing there with his mouth wide open. That was Ernie for you."

Then there was the morning of May 5, 1988, when Sirott was anchoring "Fox Thing in the Morning" with his future wife Marianne Murciano. "It was early in the season and it was kind of a wet, damp, chilly day, and it was going to be one of [Kerry] Wood's first starts. I just had a feeling about that game, and I talked about it on TV. I said I was going to go out [to Wrigley] for the game [after the show]. Nobody wanted to go with me, so I ended up going by myself. And it was around the sixth inning or so when I turned to this woman next to me who was keeping score, and I asked her, 'How many strikeouts does Wood have?' Of course, the rest is history. He strikes out 20 and it's one of the greatest games ever pitched."

Sirott was also at Wrigley on October 22, 2016, for Game 6 of the National League Championship Series, when the Cubs defeated the Dodgers 5-0 to clinch the pennant for the first time since 1945. "I happened to be sitting right behind [former Cubs catcher] Randy Hundley, and, to me, that was the greatest… to experience that with one of the guys I loved as a kid – one of the players that I really enjoyed watching and getting to know – and seeing the expression on his face."

Being a Cubs fan "has always been a very unique thing," Sirott said. "Now I'm passing on this thing called Cubs fandom to my daughter [Daniela]. When I'm at the game with her, I think about my dad taking me to the game. It's a life lesson, a generational link. It's about being loyal and, also, it's about sticking with something. It's a very special thing."

25. Bobby Skafish

There are a lot of smells that evoke a day at the ballpark – some of them pleasant, others less so. The scent of a good quality stogie, however one might feel about the habit of smoking, can be agreeable under the right circumstances. Bobby Skafish, a Chicago-area radio personality for over four decades, associates youthful Wrigley Field memories with the vapor of fans. "My earliest and most enduring Cubs memory is the smell of cigar smoke wafting through the stands at games I attended as a youngster," he said. "To this day the smell of cigar smoke conjures up memories of games at Wrigley."

Skafish, a native of Hammond, Indiana, came into the world with blue Cubbie blood running through his veins. He was "born into a Cubs-loving family," he said in an emailed exchange. "My dad and two older brothers all loved the Cubs, so I just fell into it. Cubs' broadcasts were on WGN-TV Channel 9 and the radio all season long."

Though the Skafish family didn't often make it to the North Side of Chicago, the connectivity offered by television and radio communications offered young Bobby – and fans across the country – a seat anywhere. Fitting for a professional who came to be linked with Windy City FM broadcast brands such as WXRT, WLUP and WDRV. "The Cubs are my neighborhood team and I feel proud that they are beloved worldwide," he said. "I'm excited to see Cubs fans attending and sometimes dominating the cheering during road games."

From the perspective of Skafish's luminous rock radio history, the Chicago Cubs are not unlike the music greats of the latter 20th century – able to fill almost any stadium, legions of fans across the globe and, as pertains to pre-2016 teams, consummate, erratic underdogs. It seems somehow right that standout moments in Skafish's recollection are ones absorbed through the airwaves.

He recalled watching NBCs "Game of the Week" on June 23, 1984, when the Cubs hosted the Cardinals at Wrigley Field. It would be the breakout game for second baseman Ryne Sandberg. In front of a national TV audience, the young Cub went five-for-six with two home runs and seven RBIs, lifting the team to victory. "The Sandberg Game," as it became known to devoted Cubs fans, sparked the team's legendary run to the postseason for the first time since 1945.

Sandberg is one of a few Cubs giants that loom large in Skafish's memory. Two other well-known Cubs greats have also secured deserved real estate. "I remember attending a personal appearance by Mr. Cub, Ernie Banks, at our sporting goods store in Hammond – my hometown – as a very young boy," he said. "He was as generous a person as he was a great player." Favorable opinions regarding Banks as a human and a baseball player are certainly more plentiful than the team's 1960s-era playoff appearances.

Appreciation for Sandberg and Banks notwithstanding, it's a great pitching ace who wins the coveted title of "favorite" in Bobby Skafish's personal Cubs Hall of Fame. "It has to be Greg Maddux," he concluded. "He was not physically imposing but succeeded through smarts and preparation. He was also a tremendous competitor."

Maddux was a key member of the Cubs pitching staff from 1986 to 1992, and again from 2004 to 2006. He won his first Cy Young Award with the Lovable Losers in 1992, the last year of his first tenure with the team. While a number of diehard fans consider the free agency departure of Maddux to the Atlanta Braves in 1993 the most egregious instance (among many) of pre-Epstein Cubs mismanagement, his career-ending return after the indignities of the 2003 season was a salve to many souls.

There's something about history's Cubbies – and the stadium they call home – that has a palliative effect. In times of struggle and triumph, Bobby Skafish viewed his career visits to Wrigley Field through a warmly lit lens. "Just being in Wrigley Field anytime is magical: the well-kept grounds, the atmosphere, the camaraderie of the fans," he said. "I live close enough to Wrigley Field to hear the cheers during key moments, the seventh inning stretch singing and the roar from rock concerts. All of that is special to me even if I only attend a few games per year. I'm there."

Being in the neighborhood and rocking out to "Go Cubs Go" by Steve Goodman felt a little extra sweet on November 2, 2016. For that of course is the amazing evening on which the Chicago Cubs secured their first World Series championship in 108 years. "When the Cubs won that final game in Cleveland, my daughter Cassidy and I walked east to Clark Street just to be among the crowd of celebrants," he said. "My overall feelings were joy, satisfaction and pride. So often a neighborhood conversation, or ones with Cubs fans who don't live in the neighborhood ends with a simple 'Go Cubs.'"

It's safe to assume that Skafish and his fellow celebrants exchanged more than polite pleasantries. The euphoria of a dream come true in Wrigleyville could be heard for miles across the city, orderly as the demonstrations of joy ultimately were. But the broadcaster doesn't need to walk to the corner of Addison and Clark to relive the good times. "Hearing the Cubs on radio, or watching them on TV," he said, "is sufficient for me to get deep into the feeling."

26. Michael Strautmanis

Michael Strautmanis lets his Cubs pride show, even on the South Side. In his Hyde Park office at the Obama Foundation where he serves as vice president of civic engagement, the walls are mostly bare. That makes the two front-page newspaper clippings – one from the *Sun-Times* and the other from the *RedEye* – stand out. Both are the Cubs winning the World Series.

"I've seen a lot," he explained. "I've experienced a lot. The [Cubs winning the World Series] was one of the greatest things I've ever experienced in my life. I just feel really lucky to be a Cubs fan."

When you look at what Strautmanis has seen and experienced, the depth of what the Cubs winning the World Series means to him stands out even more.

Strautmanis met Barack and Michelle Obama while still a law student at the University of Illinois in the early 1990s. He eventually worked on the campaign to elect Obama to the U.S. Senate in 2004 and then on the campaign to elect the country's first African-American president in 2008. When Obama won, he brought Strautmanis into the White House with him to serve as chief of staff to Valerie Jarrett. Now Strautmanis is the main face of the Obama Foundation in Chicago, which is developing the presidential library campus on the South Side.

"I definitely thought that Barack Obama becoming president was more likely than the Cubs winning the World Series," Strautanis chuckled. "He'd won before and the Cubs had not."

Strautmanis' relationship with the Cubs began when he was a young boy growing up in the Uptown neighborhood of Chicago, not far from Wrigley Field. His adoptive father, Juris Strautmanis, a Latvian immigrant and now retired Chicago public schools teacher, taught him what it meant to be a Cubs fan. "I think in a way that only an immigrant can, he embraced the Cubs and baseball," Strautmanis said. "He was really excited to have me experience that."

Of course, living so close to Wrigley Field and taking the Clark Street bus past the iconic stadium had an impact as well. "Geography is never just geography in Chicago," Strautmanis said. "Geography is destiny. For me it was destiny in a way that gave me a lot of opportunity. It gave me a chance to root for the Cubs and that's been a great journey."

Strautmanis, who sold T-shirts outside of Wrigley Field as a teen-ager, came to learn as he got older that as an African-American, he was a member of a "small club." As he explained, in the 90s, as an African-American, "it was cool to be a White Sox fan; it was not cool to be a Cubs fan."

"It was like I was not really black, and I was a fan of a terrible losing team," Strautmanis said. "I actually think that in a way I started to really embrace that as something that was unique and different about me."

After the Cubs clinched the pennant for the first time since 1945, in a game that Strautmanis attended with his wife, Damona, he wrote in an essay for *The Undefeated* that there's "nothing blacker than being a Cubs fan."

"What I meant is that I have always felt that embracing my identity as an African-American has been a part of embracing the challenges, embracing the pain, embracing the struggle," he explained.

"I know it's sports and sports are not as serious as life, but sports is a metaphor and that's one of the reasons why we love it so much. We have these dramas that play out on these fields. Owning and embracing the fact that my favorite team lost and would lose and would often lose in painful ways… In many ways, it would seem hopeless. My Cubs never really had a chance and it seemed like [African-Americans] were never really going to have a chance.

"Yet there is, I think, within the African-American tradition and the African-American community, hope. And that is something that I've embraced as well. I had a chance to see that come to life in what I watched with President Obama. Even though that was an amazing experience, it fit within what I've been taught my entire life. Whether it was about the civil rights movement or the journey of my own personal family. It was one of pain and struggle and setback, but also success and triumph and overcoming."

Strautmanis' hope now is that more African-Americans will embrace the team that has meant so much to him. "It would be fun to have Wrigley Field look like America," he said. "I love this team. I love this country. My hope is that we can overcome some of the natural barriers that may be a part of our city. There are great things about our city – I love the city of Chicago – but there are some things I think we need to leave behind. And maybe this North Side-South Side divide about the Cubs and the White Sox is one of them."

27. Steve Trout

Steve Trout is the rare Cubs fan who started as a White Sox fan. Growing up in South Holland, about 20 miles south of Chicago, Trout was practically raised in the old Comiskey Park. His father, Dizzy Trout pitched for 14 years in the major leagues. The two-time All-Star led the league in wins in 1943 and in ERA in 1944. After being released by the Baltimore Orioles in 1957 at the age of 42, he joined the Chicago White Sox as a pitching instructor and then worked with that organization's front office for several years.

"[Comiskey Park] was my playground" as a child, Steve Trout said. "So, of course, I was a White Sox fan. I was a baseball fan, but because of my dad, I only really knew the White Sox."

Following in the footsteps of his father, Trout, nicknamed "Rainbow," became a big-league pitcher himself, hurling for four teams – the Chicago White Sox, the Chicago Cubs, the New York Yankees, and the Seattle Mariners – over the course of a 12-year career.

"I was not a Cubs fan," Trout recalled. "I never went to Wrigley Field. I didn't even know how to get there when I got traded to them."

As it turned out, his best year came with the Cubs, in 1984, when he went 13-7 in 31 starts, posting a 3.41 ERA, helping the North Siders to their first postseason berth since 1945, when they lost against a Tigers team anchored by Trout's father. Trout pitched the Cubs to victory in Game 2 of the 1984 National League Championship Series against the San Diego Padres, going 8.1 strong innings. That put the Cubs one victory away from their first World Series since 1945. But that one victory never came, as the Padres swept the next three games, stealing from Trout the chance to go to the World Series and face the American League champion Tigers, the team on which his father had pitched 39 years earlier against the Cubs.

That lost opportunity to pitch in a Cubs-Tigers World Series just as his father had done in 1945 still aches a bit. "It was one of the great, great stories…the Cubs back in the World Series playing against the Detroit Tigers, the last team to play them in the World Series – and the son of the guy who beat them would be playing for the other team," Trout said. "It was this incredible story that unfortunately never got to be told."

Now 27 years after he pitched his last game in the majors, though he still roots for the Sox, Trout's baseball allegiances have swung more to the North Side, to the team that he almost pitched into the World Series. "I think I became a fan when they invited me back into their arms, particularly with Tom Ricketts," he said. "When the Ricketts family bought the team, we had lunch and he wanted to hear my story. He wanted to talk to me about my dad. After lunch, he was thankful that we got to meet. I just really thought that this guy had the vision, the love, the passion for baseball – Cubs baseball and Cubs people. We've seen since that that is all true."

Along with his former teammate from that 1984 team, Hall of Famer Ryne Sandberg, among other former players, Trout now serves as a Cubs ambassador. When he's not at Wrigley Field, Trout has shared his passion for baseball with youngsters by teaching instructional baseball clinics for youths at Oz Park in Chicago's Lincoln Park neighborhood and at Kerry Wood Cubs Field in Roscoe Village. He also recently brought his love of the game into print, with the publication of a children's book, *Loosey-Goosey Baseball,* co-authored by Marlene Matthias and illustrated by Steve Feldman. In it, "Coach Rainbow" teaches lessons about youth baseball not just for young ballplayers but for their parents as well.

Trout finally made it to the World Series in 2016, but as a fan. He was there at Wrigley for Games 3 through 5, which stirred up some mixed emotions as he thought about what could have been in 1984. "You know how close you were to being there," he said. "It doesn't take away from your happiness for [the 2016 Cubs] but it makes you think more about what could have been. There's so much that goes into getting there, and when you don't get there…all the pain and hard work that goes into that, the up and down life, and then when you don't get there. Then you watch this, and you're just so happy for the players and the people who work there and for the fans. But you really wanted to be on that field with that success of winning."

The former pitcher credits Cubs owner Tom Ricketts for having both the vision and the plan to make the dream a reality. "He wanted to bring the Lovable Losers mentality to an end and to make them into the Lovable Winners," Trout said, "and that's what he did."

28. Scott Turow

A third-generation Cubs fan, author Scott Turow had come to believe that, like his father and grandfather before him, he would never see the Cubs win a World Series.

Turow's father, born David Turowetsky, was the "Cubs-fan-in-chief" in the family. He told the story of his father, a Russian-Jewish immigrant who came to Chicago and fell for the game of baseball and the North Side team. Friendships hung on every pitch. "[My grandfather and his best friend] would listen to the ballgame on the radio and then they would run out between innings and they would yell at each other over the fence in Yiddish about what was going on in the ballgame, and then they would run back upstairs."

"My father rooted for this team his whole life," Turow said during an interview at a coffee shop a couple blocks from his home on the North Shore. "He died without ever seeing them win."

The 68-year-old best-selling author whose 1987 debut novel, *Presumed Innocent*, spawned the legal thriller genre, caught the Cubs' bug early on. "There's a picture of me as a five-year-old in a Cubs uniform," he said.

Like most of the kids in his neighborhood, he worshiped Ernie Banks. "I think every kid my age learned to hit with their right elbow parallel to the ground."

He was 20 when he witnessed the Cubs collapse in

1969, when a black cat infamously waltzed around Cubs third baseman Ron Santo as he stood in the on-deck circle during a game at Shea Stadium against the New York Mets. "I was too young to have accepted this idea that they would never win," he recalled, "but it was heartbreaking. It was like watching somebody die on the cross."

All but one of his 11 novels are set in Kindle County, Turow's fictional version of Chicago, where a hapless professional baseball team, the Trappers, bear a mighty resemblance to the Cubs of old. "It's a lovely motif to have all of this futility," he said of the fictional counterpart to the Lovable Losers.

After watching an easy grounder roll between first baseman Leon Durham's legs during the 1984 National League Championship Series and then a bespectacled fan reach for a foul ball that looked like it would land in left fielder Moises Alou's glove in 2003, Turow had come to not only expect but to accept losing as a way of life for his favorite baseball team. "I had begun to believe that, like my father, I was going to die without ever seeing the Cubs play in the World Series," he said.

"Being a Cubs fan was pretty much unique because you knew they were, in the end, always going to lose and it was a testimonial to hope and faith and loyalty."

As he once told a reporter, "It's character-building when the Cubs stomp on your heart and you have to put it back in your chest."

In 2016, when the Cubs finally did make it to the Fall Classic, Turow was there, with his son, for Game 3, the first World Series game played at Wrigley Field since 1945. Fittingly, the Cubs lost 1-0 to the Cleveland Indians, to fall behind 2-1 in the Series. Still, just to be there, at a World Series game, at Wrigley Field, and to experience it with his son, was something truly special.

Then came Game 7, which he started to watch at a party with friends. Turow claimed that he remained "perfectly calm" when the Indians' light-hitting outfielder Rajai Davis hit the game-tying two-run homer off Cubs' fireballer Aroldis Chapman in the bottom of the eighth inning. "I knew that if this was ever going to happen," he said, "it wasn't going to be easy."

As he later wrote in an essay for *Time Magazine*, he believed because his "inner six-year-old has always had to."

When the grounds crew rolled out the tarp, Turow went home, where he watched the end of the game. After Cubs' third baseman Kris Bryant scooped up that grounder and slipped on the wet grass as he threw, and the ball landed safely in the outstretched mitt of first baseman Anthony Rizzo, Turow knew that hope had finally won over futility.

"I know exactly what I did at that moment," he said. "I went out the back door. I fell on my knees. And I screamed as loud as I could: 'It finally happened!'"

For Turow, the Cubs winning the World Series "means that if you live long enough, anything can happen."

Does that mean that there's still hope for his fictional Trappers? The author cracked a sly smile at the question. "That would be an imprudent use of literary license to leave the Trappers in despair," he said.

29. Ronnie "Woo Woo" Wickers

Ronnie "Woo Woo" Wickers has been a fixture at Wrigley Field for half a century, nearly as long as the ivy on the outfield walls. With "Ronnie Woo Woo" stitched onto the back of his Cubs uniform, he is, next to Kris Bryant or Anthony Rizzo, probably the most recognizable character at the Friendly Confines. And if you put aside the big-name celebrities like Eddie Vedder and Bill Murray, Wickers is arguably the most famous Cubs fan alive today. In the bleachers and on the streets, he's typically in high demand with fans and tourists asking to pose for pictures with him.

He is known to Wrigley Field visitors for his signature cheers at baseball games, punctuated with an exclamatory "Woo!" The National Bobblehead Hall of Fame and Museum even honored Wickers with his own wooing bobblehead.

"Every true Chicagoan knows who he is," his daughter, Yolanda Linneman, said in an email interview. "His good spirit makes people want to be around him."

Though he grew up on the South Side, he became attached to Wrigley Field, the place where his grandmother had taken him to see Jackie Robinson play. The Cubs' logo looked a lot like his favorite teddy bear.

"My mom would always say you can make all the noise you want [at the ballpark]," he said during an interview at an Italian restaurant on the North Side.

Wickers took his mother's words to heart and started wooing at Wrigley in 1957 or 1958, when he was just a teen. "It was something that just caught on," he said.

In 2005, filmmaker Paul Hoffman released a documentary film about Wickers, called *WooLife*, in which he explained his ballpark cheers. "It's a rejoice," he said then. "It's a happiness. It's a feeling that I can't really explain. I want people to know that it's a song all over the universe when you hear Ronnie Woo Woo."

That film brought out into the light the struggles Wickers had been facing outside of the ballpark. After the deaths of both his grandmother and girlfriend in the 1980s, a distraught Wickers found himself homeless and without a stable job.

The character he plays at Wrigley in many ways masks who he really is. For many years, he'd disappear at night into a cardboard box. Wrigley and the Cubs and their fans were his escape from his cold reality. When he wore that uniform, he had superhero powers that at least for a few hours a day made him feel pure joy.

Wrigley Field has always been his "getaway," explained Linneman. "For him, there's no better feeling than the positive vibes around the ballpark and the smell of hot dogs. He loves making people smile."

Yet the good feelings between Wickers and the Cubs have not always been mutual. While Wickers has had many backers, including ex-Cubs like Hall of Famer Andre Dawson who once donated his shoes to the famous fan, he has also had his share of detractors. Some fans see him as nothing more than an annoying ballpark clown, and Cubs management has through the years not always been receptive to his antics.

For years he'd wanted to sing "Take Me Out to the Ball Game" as a guest conductor during the seventh-inning stretch at Wrigley Field as hundreds of celebrities had done. After initially resisting the idea of letting Wickers take the microphone, Cubs management finally relented and on May 24, 2001, he became the first regular fan to serve as guest conductor.

That seemed to thaw relations at least temporarily. But early in the 2017 season, as the Cubs were struggling out of the gate following their championship season, a front-page story broke in the *Sun-Times*. Columnist Mary Mitchell wrote that Wickers had claimed that Cubs security booted him from an April 19 game for entering the ballpark without a ticket – an allegation that Wickers vehemently denies to this day (he claims that he entered the bleachers using an e-ticket that was on a friend's smart phone). Though the dust has since somewhat settled, Wickers contends that Cubs security singled him out. The Cubs, meanwhile, insist that they were in the right to remove the long-time fan when he didn't produce a ticket.

Despite his claims of mistreatment at the hands of Cubs security and management, Wickers remains unwavering in his support and loyalty to the Cubs. All that he wants is for the team to embrace him the same way he's embraced the team. "He's cheered for this team all these years," said Janet Tabit, his friend and confidante, "and they've done almost nothing for him in return."

As luck would have it, Wickers missed the second half of the 2016 championship run after suffering a knee injury in a fall in the bleachers for which he underwent reconstructive surgery. Still, he hobbled in a brace to the Holiday Club, at Irving Park and Sheridan, to watch Game 7.

"When they won I couldn't jump up and down like I wanted to," he said. "But just to see it…it was amazing. I always wanted the Cubs to win the World Series, and I always believed that one day they would win it."

His chant isn't nearly as loud as it once was. But at 75, he's still sharp. He can reel off the names of Cubs players from when he became a fan and first started his iconic woo back in the late '50s and early '60s. "Dee Fondy. Dee Fondy Woo. Hank Sauer. Hank Sauer Woo. Dick Drought. Dick Drought Woo."

"Whatever happens in my life," he said, "[the Cubs] will always have a place in my heart."

30. Kathy Wolter Mondelli

Kathy Wolter Mondelli was, in her own words, one of the *other* Cubs ballgirls.

The ballgirl was Marla Collins. If you were male and a Cubs fan in the 1980s, you probably remember Collins. Heck, you probably fantasized about her. Maybe you still do.

From 1982 to 1986, the team paid Collins $150 per game to retrieve foul balls while wearing a Cubs uniform that included extra-short shorts for those hot summer days. The late, great Cubs broadcaster Harry Caray was one of Collins' biggest fans and would often be distracted from the game by her. Some viewers found this habit of his annoying if not disturbing. But it was what made Harry different from most every other sports broadcaster out there. He was genuine and never pretended to be anything other than what he was.

The Cubs fired Collins in the middle of a dismal 1986 season after she posed nude for *Playboy* magazine. According to *Chicago Tribune* columnist Fred Mitchell, she was fired for breaking the "family-oriented spirit" of the Cubs.

In a 1989 interview with the *Chicago Tribune*, Collins observed the irony of the Cubs hiring and putting her in the shortest of shorts, and then firing her for taking them off. "You don't put anyone with lots of curves in real short shorts and a tight shirt if you don't want her noticed."

No, you don't. The reality was that Collins was oftentimes

as popular if not more popular than the players. The Cubs knew that, which is why they went looking for a replacement for her.

Enter Wolter Mondelli and Mariellen Kopp, dubbed by Harry Caray "The Blonde" and "The Brunette," respectively. The pair took over for Collins in the second half of the 1986 season and stayed on for 1987. They weren't asked to return the following season.

"I did ask why ballgirls were no longer going to be hired, and the organization stated they would be utilizing the batboys instead," Wolter Mondelli wrote in an email. "It's my opinion that there was too much controversy with regards to *Playboy* and they didn't want that to be synonymous with baseball, apple pie and the Cubs."

Wolter Mondelli, who now works as a stand-in on the NBC crime drama *Chicago P.D.*, when she's not hanging out at La Scarola, the family's West Loop Italian restaurant, has nothing but fond memories of her brief stint as Cubs ballgirl.

"It was surreal," Wolter Mondelli said in a phone interview. "Totally surreal. All Cubs fans know that incredible feeling you get rooting for your team. To be able to get to be closer to the players and more involved in the game…it was kind of a dream come true.

"To be on that field is just really hard to explain. It was dream-like. Every time I walked through the dugout and every time I was able to be there for the National Anthem and to walk out onto the field and to stay there for the game…the entire time it felt as if I was on a cloud, in a dream. It truly did. It was that terrific."

One of her most memorable experiences came in just her second game. "Daryl Strawberry hit a foul ball and I actually felt the brush of wind as it passed my face," she wrote in an email. "It was terrifying as well as exciting, and I thought, 'Wow, I'm in the big leagues here!'"

For Wolter Mondelli, the Cubs fan came before the ballgirl. As a young girl growing up on the North Side, she would go to games with her grandmother. "My grandmother, in her sixties, knew every single players' stats; she knew everything about them. She would give you their height, their weight, just everything there was to know about them. And then she would talk about it with all the other Cubs fans around her."

One of her best childhood memories was sitting at a Cubs game and having popcorn rain down upon her when the crowd jumped to celebrate. Now when she goes to games, she and her sister, Lori Myers, always make sure to have a box of popcorn at the ready. "We call it popcorn fireworks," Wolter Mondelli said. "We always make sure to buy popcorn. We don't eat it; we just have it for when something good happens during the game. We throw it up in the air because it's my hope that some little kid is going to be sitting there, and popcorn is going to come down on them and they're going to have that same feeling that I did."

Wolter Mondelli watched Game 7 of the 2016 World Series at home with family and friends. When the Cubs won, "I just remember closing my eyes and thinking that it actually happened. It actually happened. The greatest thing ever. Then of course, I thought back to all those people who missed it. We all have those people who we're sorry were not around to see it. My grandfather. My grandmother. My mom. First, I was happy. Then I closed my eyes and thought about them."

31. Adrian Zmed

Adrian Zmed has sustained a movie, television and stage career for over four decades. A reputation as something of a Renaissance Man who can dance, sing, play musical instruments and tell a funny story creates endless opportunities. Zmed is also a renowned and unapologetic diehard Chicago Cubs fan. He recalled his first trip to Wrigley Field – a place he calls "home" – as a small child.

"I went to my first game with my older brother Cornel when I was four years old and I fell in love," he said. "We sat in the center field bleachers. Wrigley is the place. The first house I ever lived in Chicago is now a teacher's parking lot. But I always have that park. I feel content and comfortable when I'm there."

Zmed's diverse entertainment career has made him something of a gypsy. At the time of this interview, the performer had just returned from London, where he appeared as George in a traveling production of La Cage Aux Folles. No matter where the road takes him however, baseball is never far from his heart. Among many endeavors, Zmed was a long-time member of the Hollywood All-Stars, a baseball team of TV actors that in 1991 included Richard Dean Anderson, Larry Drake, Jason Priestley and Kelsey Grammer. One glorious day, during Zmed's early years with the team, they took the field against the 1969 Cubs. The superfan could hardly believe his luck.

"I was going to meet Ernie, Ron and Billy!" he recalled. "During their heyday, I was one of the kids who hung around outside Wrigley with my glove. I actually picked up four balls. So when I found out the All-Stars were going to play the '69 guys, I asked my mom for those old balls. She had thrown them away. She thought I outgrew them. But that's okay. I was lucky enough to have plenty of chances to meet them."

The 1969 Chicago Cubs team is special to Zmed, September slide notwithstanding. In fact, he credits Ernie, Ron, Billy, et al. with saving his life.

"I broke my leg playing football in 1968," he said. "I was 14 years old. It was so bad I had to get the leg rebroken and reset and I was in a body cast. I laid in bed for months at my house at Seminary and Belden. The 1969 Cubs kept me alive and excited – and away from depression. Jack Brickhouse and that voice. The team was so electrifying. They would pull out ninth-inning stuff beyond belief. Of course, everything collapsed in September and that was hard. I will never forgive the Mets for waving their handkerchiefs at us. But I will always be grateful to the 1969 Cubs team."

While Santo, Banks and Williams were certainly the standout stars of the late 1960s Cubs, and Zmed counted himself among their many fans, second baseman Glenn Beckert also made an impression on the young boy. Beckert played nine seasons with the Cubbies from 1965 to 1973 and took time to meet with kids in the community throughout his stay.

"Glenn Beckert visited my grammar school, Oscar Mayer, when I was a student," he recalled. "He was a nice guy and I always liked the way he played. He was underrated, approachable, a .290 hitter and a great defensive man. Everyone loved Ernie Banks, right? He was all heart, the greatest guy on earth. I still love him and my heart broke when he died. But I also liked Beckert. He got less attention, but he also had a sense of humor and a flair for the dramatic. When the Hollywood All-Stars played the '69 Cubs, Beckert was there too. He kind of did a Babe Ruth on me. He pointed to me, and then hit a line drive at me. I loved it."

Zmed has developed and maintained many relationships within the Cubs organization over the course of his long career. He spoke highly of Ron Santo and his transition from player to media professional. "I loved what Santo brought to the broadcast booth – just a fan yelling from his living room like all the other fans. He felt what we felt."

Despite his closeness over the years with the 1969 gang, as well as later Cub greats, including Mark Grace and Rick Sutcliffe, Zmed never lost the childlike wonder. "No matter what else I accomplished, I was the team's water boy. I never lost that sense of magic no matter what my personal relationship was with the players."

The entertainer was a steadfast team loyalist through many lean years. But there was still that one thing he waited for.

"A Cubs World Series Championship was number one on my bucket list," he said. "When the team finally won, I thought 'I can move on with my life or die. It doesn't matter.' I've done everything I ever wanted to do in my life."

Zmed vividly recalled that dramatic ending to Game 7. "I was at O'Hare Airport – of all places – when the rain delay came," he said. "As the drops started falling, I figured maybe that was it. Another bad sign. I was happy we'd come that close. I had the game on my laptop as my wife, dog and I sat at a wine bar. It was very late. But a crowd gathered behind us. Eventually I had to shut down my computer for boarding.

"We were on the plane when the game ended, and people were crying. I saw the rain delay in a new way. I felt like Ernie Banks and Harry Caray went to God and said, 'We have to stop this. The rain drops are the tears of 108 years of disappointment. These guys need to go back to the dugout and regroup.' It was a divine intervention that flipped the switch. The Cubs were a different team when they came back to the field."

To complete the religious metaphor, Zmed likens the subsequent World Series celebration to a pilgrimage. He observed of the estimated five million people who descended upon the Windy City, "It takes the Cubs and Gandhi to draw crowds that size. It takes a miracle."

NEW! 2019
Expanded Edition Stories

Photo by *Blake Guidry* on Unsplash.com

32. Brian Bernardoni

2019 marks Brian Bernardoni's 22nd season as a part-time Wrigley Field tour guide. In that time, he estimates that he has led tens of thousands of fans on at least 600 tours of the Friendly Confines. He's not missed a season since he started in 1998.

"I'm the oldest of the tour guides now – I'm 51," Bernardoni said during an interview at his home in a suburb southwest of Chicago. "I'm one of the longest-tenured tour guides."

Why does he keep coming back, year after year? "It's love," he said. "I still get giddy. I get to sell joy. I never for a single day forget that I get to not only talk about Wrigley Field, but I get to be on that field. It's that childhood dream."

For Bernardoni, who spends his weekdays working as a lobbyist for realtors, that childhood dream starts at daybreak on the weekends when he's giving tours of his favorite place. "I get there usually two or three hours early. I go down to the infield and the grounds grew is usually there, and I'll rake the infield with them," said Bernardoni. "It's calming for me. The longer I've been there, the more I've learned about hard work than I've ever learned in my 35 years in politics – about dedication, attention to detail, teamwork – all of that I see just from the grounds crew. I get to have those little life experiences. When the fans come in, it's different – it's showtime."

On every one of his tours, Bernardoni begins by reciting from a 1948 article that appeared in *The Evening Post* about one of the most legendary moments in Wrigley Field's history: Babe Ruth's "called shot" during the 1932 World Series.

"As long as baseball is played, the memory will live of a bulbous man on matchstick leg pointing in eloquent gesture towards Wrigley Field's faraway centerfield barrier, the jibes of 50,000 Chicago fans searing his ears," Bernardoni's booming voice echoes.

"There are two strikes on George Herman 'Babe' Ruth, like there'd been many times in his career. The score was 4 to 4 in the fifth inning and Ruth's Yankees were gunning for their third straight win. Two called strikes and there stood baseball's greatest hitter in the sunset of his career, majestically drawing a bead on a spot some 400 feet away. Contemptuously, the Babe held up two fingers and pointed to the centerfield flagpole.

"Charley Root pitched. He shouldn't have done it. Like a projectile the ball left the Ruthian bat to scream on a line over the right centerfield barrier."

Bernardoni then pauses, and for the first time, he looks at the fans on the tour. "I haven't even introduced myself," he said. "I spend the next five minutes ripping that story to shreds."

"You set up the tour in such a way that you've got to have command, that you are in a place of respect," Bernardoni said. "This is a cathedral of baseball…but baseball is full of bullshit and there are stories that are just not true or are not accurate, and [the 'called shot'] is one of them."

Bernardoni's grandmother, Emily Kwiatek Bernardoni, played second base for a women's softball team at Wrigley Field in 1933. "My history [with Wrigley Field] is first person," he said. "My oldest daughter, Genevieve, who is 20, actually took her first step in short center field, just a few feet away from where her great-grandmother played. That is the kind of the linkage to me being part of the Cubs."

Said Bernardon: "There are other things that I love, things that most fans don't get to see…I love watching the sunrise at the ballpark, I love hearing the birds, I love watching the grounds crew, I love the architecture, I love the slope, I love the lines…I love the fact that it's a mosaic – that so many different architects have touched that ballpark and whatever that snapshot of time is, that first time you see the ballpark is what Wrigley Field will always be to you… but because I've been so intimately involved, it's grown around me too. I still get excited about it – there's something about that place. It's home to me."

Though he is a Wrigley Field historian, Bernardoni said he is, first and foremost, a fan. "I live and die [with the Cubs] like every other [Cubs] fan does," he said.

Bernardoni grew up in Garfield Ridge, on Chicago's southwest side – yes, in White Sox territory. "Part of it was being a rebel," he said. "I was a southwest sider, but I wanted to be different."

He now lives in his grandparents' house with his wife, Carrie, and their three daughters. Just how big a part of his life are the Cubs? Well, Ernie Banks – aka "Mr. Cub" – introduced him to his wife. Pat Brickhouse, the widow of famed Cubs' broadcaster Jack Brickhouse, toasted them at their wedding. The house is like a museum, with a den and self-described "man cave" that are decorated with historic relics of Wrigley Field and pre-Wrigley Field ball fields where the Cubs played.

"I've got seven or eight file cabinets of the history of Wrigley Field," he said. "Those things are facts to me – they are moments of time." They include menus, postcards, blueprints, contracts, photos, scorecards, and press releases. He's never counted but estimates that he probably has "a thousand artifacts of note. There are some that I've worked really hard to obtain."

Bernardoni has no idea what the dollar value of his collection would be. To him, they're priceless. One day, he said, he will likely donate the bulk of the collection to the National Baseball Hall of Fame and Museum in Cooperstown, New York.

Being a Cubs fan, he said, "It means love, it means

passion, it means criticism, it means pain and suffering, it means joy, it means family to me. My real family tolerates that I have a love for my baseball family."

When the rain delay came during Game 7 of the 2016 World Series, Bernardoni put his middle daughter Ceci, who was then 10 and already a die-hard Cubs fan, to bed, because she had school the next morning. "I remember rehearsing in my head, 'Sweetheart, this is what happens when you're a Cubs fan, we'll get them next year.' I'm so glad I didn't have to give my daughter that speech."

Of all his baseball possessions, the one Bernardoni prizes the most is the World Series ring that Cubs owner Tom Ricketts gave to him after the team's historic win. "I couldn't have been more stunned when I got the ring," he said.

The only hiccup was that his last name was misspelled on the ring. It wasn't long before he got a new one with the correct spelling. He freely shares it with anyone who wants to try it on – though he makes sure to get it back from them. "When I do an event, I'm very happy to share the ring," he said. "While the ring belongs to my family, I've never said no to a Cubs fan who has wanted to wear it. We've gone so long to get that ring…I'm not a member of the 2016 Cubs…I'm not anything other than a guy who just happened to be lucky enough to get the ring. You don't get to meet those people too often in life, so if they see me with my ring, I let them wear it…let them see the goat on the inside, let them feel the weight of the ring…let them share in it."

33. Jose Cardenal

José Rosario Domec Cardenal always dreamt that one day he'd play for his favorite Major League Baseball team, the Chicago Cubs. "That was the team I wanted to play for since I was a little kid," the 77-year-old said in a phone interview.

A lot of kids have that dream but only a handful see it come true. Imagine the odds of realizing such a dream if you were growing up in Cuba. Yet Cardenal did just that. Though the route he took to get there was anything but direct or easy.

The youngest of five, Cardenal was born in Matanzas, Cuba, on October 7, 1943, to a carpenter father and homemaker mother. He is the second cousin of former Athletics shortstop Bert Campaneris, and they grew up a few blocks apart in Matanzas; they would often play baseball together.

Cardenal was only 16 when he left Cuba on March 23, 1960, to come to play baseball in the United States, one of the last Cuban baseball players to leave that island before the Fidel Castro regime clamped down following the Cuban Revolution in 1959. According to an article written for the Society for American Baseball Research, Cardenal spent the $200 signing bonus he received from the San Francisco Giants to purchase a suit, a pair of shoes, and a new baseball glove.

The outfielder spent most of the next four years in the

Giants' minor league system. Even though he seemed ready for the big leagues by 1964, San Francisco didn't have a place for him with a strong outfield that featured future Hall of Famer Willie Mays and two of the Alou brothers, Jesus and Matty. The following season, he was sent to Los Angeles, where he played for the Angels for the next three years. Then he bounced around from Cleveland to St. Louis to Milwaukee before finally landing, in 1972, in the place he wanted to be.

"For me Wrigley Field was like a paradise," Cardenal said. "This was the first time I saw ivy around the outfield, and that was beautiful. Then to see people in the ballpark just screaming to you from the stands, it was great, especially when we played St. Louis. When we played St. Louis, that was our World Series."

What he most enjoyed about being in Chicago was that, at the time, all the games were played during the day. "It was great to play in Chi-Town," Cardenal said. "The thing that I really enjoyed is that by five you were home because there were no lights. After the game was over, you'd just go home."

In his first three seasons (1972-74) as a Cub, the right-handed hitting outfielder had arguably his three most productive seasons in the Major Leagues, hitting .290 or better each season. His best year roaming the Cubs outfield was 1973 when he led the team in hitting (.303), doubles (33), and steals (19) and was named the Chicago Player of the Year by the city's baseball writers.

Known for the Afro haircut that stuck out of the sides of his cap, basket catches, and unusual injuries (he refused to play the opener in 1974 claiming that he was injured because the eyelids of one eye were stuck open), Cardenal became a fan favorite.

"I used to sign autographs to anybody and take pictures," said Cardenal, explaining partly what made him so popular.

As a player, Cardenal compared himself to the Cubs' current star, Javier Baez. "I used to be like Baez," Cardenal said. "Baez reminds me of myself when I was playing. He's a very flashy ballplayer and he can do anything to win the game. That's the kind of ballplayer I was. The only difference is that Baez has more power than me – and he makes a lot more money."

What is perhaps most telling is that Cardenal's popularity has lasted and made him into somewhat of a Cubs' version of Forrest Gump.

After the Cubs won the World Series in 2016, President Obama invited the championship team to the White House for a ceremony honoring their historic title. Cardenal was surprised to learn that he too was on the guest list. He was at the annual Cubs Convention in Chicago when the team's traveling secretary approached him with the news.

"He said to me, 'Jose, tomorrow we're going to the White House in Washington to meet the president,' and he said, 'Are you coming with us?' I said, 'Why, do I have to go? You people won the trophy. I said, No, no, no, no, no.

"He said, 'Jose, the lady requests you.' I said, 'What lady?' He said, 'The first lady, Michelle Obama, she wants you to be there because you're her idol.'

"So, I said, 'I guess I have no choice. I have to go.' The next day I had the opportunity to meet [the first lady], and she came to me, and she hugged me, and she told me the whole story that when she was a kid and I was her idol. The Cubs players looked at me and said, 'Jose, you the man.' I said, 'I don't know if I'm the man, but I'm the lady's idol,' and she became a good friend to me."

At a private reception, President Obama, whose allegiances to the South Side White Sox are well-known, explained how his wife grew up a Cubs fan and that her favorite player was Cardenal. "Back then he had a big Afro, and she was describing how she would try to wear her hat over her Afro the same way Jose did," the president said.

Added the president: "Jose Cardenal, who got the longest hug from the first lady we've ever seen – her favorite player of all time – you're the MVP today."

Cardenal has also gotten the rock star treatment, developing a close friendship with Pearl Jam frontman Eddie Vedder. As a teen, Vedder, who grew up in Evanston a die-hard Cubs fan, would hang out after the games and talk with Cardenal. The two met again in 2002, when Cardenal was a coach with the Cincinnati Reds, who were at Wrigley for a game. A batboy approached Cardenal and told him that Vedder wanted to meet him. The band was standing behind home plate. Cardenal didn't even know who Vedder was and mistakenly went up to the band's bass player, who laughed and pointed Cardenal to Vedder.

"He came to me and he hugged me. He told me, 'Do you remember that guy who used to be waiting for you and blah, blah, blah…?' I said, 'No.' He said, 'Well it was me.' Since that day, we just got along. He's my real hero now. He told me you never know who you're dealing with. He was a kid and that kid turned out to be a great musician."

Vedder has worn Cardenal's No. 1 jersey when his band has played at Wrigley Field, sung "Take Me Out to the Ballgame" with Cardenal during the seventh-inning stretch, and brought the former Cub on the stage with him at times.

Said Cardenal: "You never know who you're going to meet, so you treat everybody with respect and love and then that's what you're going to get back. That's exactly what happened [with Vedder]."

Cardenal played six of his 18 seasons in the Major Leagues with the Cubs but never even made it to the postseason with them, let alone the World Series. So, when the team finally won it all in 2016, he said, "I got a tear in my eye. That's what I wanted to do for the Cubs when I was a player, but I never had the opportunity. But I feel right now that I'm very happy and glad that finally, after so many years, they made it because I was told for so many years to wait until next year, wait until next year…finally after so many years my dream came true. It was a great feeling, a great feeling."

34. Bob Dernier

Bob Dernier's all-time favorite Cubs team used to be the 1984 squad that he played for. That team holds a special place in his heart – as it does for many Cub fans. The fleet-footed center fielder (nicknamed "The Deer") played a pivotal part as the leadoff-hitting sparkplug for that National League East championship team. Hall of Fame second baseman Ryne Sandberg batted second and the lead-off pair was dubbed "The Daily Double" by Cubs announcer Harry Caray. Dernier won the Gold Glove that season. He homered leading off the first inning of Game 1 in the 1984 National League Championship Series to kick off a 13-0 victory for the Cubs. The North Siders took Game 2, but they dropped the next three games against the Padres in San Diego, to lose the series three games to two.

The lasting image of that 1984 season for many Cubs fans is the ball rolling through first baseman Leon Durham's legs in the bottom of the seventh inning of the deciding Game 5 to help put the Padres on top for good.

"That was a long flight home," Dernier acknowledged in a phone interview.

The 1984 Cubs stand out in the team's history as the team that snapped the franchise's ugly 39-year stretch without an appearance in the postseason. That is reason enough to count them as one of the most beloved Cubs' teams of all time. They finished the regular season with a 96-65 record, 31 games over .500, after having ended the previous season 20 games below the .500 mark – a remarkable turnaround that awoke a fan base to the belief that winning was possible.

Dernier played three more seasons with the Cubs, but they didn't make it back to the postseason again until after he left. The team couldn't overcome injuries to its starting rotation in 1985, and struggles continued in 1986. Then it hit rock bottom when the team finished last in 1987, Dernier's last as a Cub.

For the players on that 1984 team, a special bond was built from that magical season that ended so painfully. "It becomes a small fraternity," Dernier said. "Sarge [the nickname of 1984 Cubs outfielder Gary Matthews] and I talk just about every other day. I see or talk to several [former 1984 teammates] regularly. When you had a significant team like that was, we all keep that with us."

The 62-year-old outfielder had a major league career that spanned 10 years (1980-1989) during which he batted .255, hit 23 homers, and stole 218 bases. He was a member of the 1983 Phillies team, which won the National League pennant but lost the World Series to the Baltimore Orioles.

Dernier didn't start out a Cubs fan. He grew up in Kansas City, the town that he still calls home. As a child, his team was the now defunct Kansas City Athletics.

Yet he has kept close ties with the Cubs organization. He

served as the team's minor league outfield and baserunning coordinator from 2007 to 2010, and then as the Cubs major league first base coach from 2010 to 2012. Now he is one of many ex-Cub players who serve a role as a team ambassador.

In October 2016, Dernier teamed with sportscaster Lou Cannelis to host Fox 32 WFLD's pregame show, *Blue October*, in conjunction with the Cubs advancing to the National League playoffs. When the Cubs reached the World Series for the first time since 1945, the station added veteran broadcaster Chip Caray, the grandson of legendary Cubs' announcer Harry Caray, to the mix.

The trio also broadcast a postgame show, putting Dernier as close as anyone who wasn't on the field to witness history unfold. "I was standing in the concourse, right up behind [Cubs first baseman Anthony] Rizzo, actually sitting up on a concession stand so that I could see. I had to hit the field as soon as the game was over to do the post-game interviews. When Bryant threw the ball and Anthony's arms went in the air, I could see right away I wasn't going down that aisle because that's where all the Cubs fans were just dancing like crazy."

Dernier beat his more experienced broadcast partners onto the field by hustling over to the other side of the stadium and entering on the third base side, which had emptied because it had been filled with fans of the losing Cleveland Indians. "That was so joyful," Dernier said. "I was so happy, and I got to share it right there on the field with a number of people. Being in all that energy made me really reflective. I had the flashback to '84 and that whole energy. It was such a relief for so many people. I was just so happy once that happened.

"We had a blast that night," Dernier said. "Ryno [Sandberg] and I ended up walking out of the stadium at 2:30 in the morning."

Just like that Dernier had a new all-time favorite Cubs team. "I would hear it year after year from the fans, that we [the 1984 Cubs] were their favorite team, and now we're their second favorite team. I'm right with them. That's a pretty good shelf to be in, so we get to soak in that."

In January 2019, the Cubs held their 34th annual Cubs Convention. Dernier was there as always – he claims to have missed it only twice. "It's a reunion, and it's a constant," he said. "I always feel like I'm in my own gym. I hope I always have that feeling when I go up there."

The Cubs and their fans have a unique and special relationship, Dernier said. "Not every big-league team has this generational reach-back where you can go back a hundred years and there are still grandmas and grandpas on the planet. You look at grandsons with Rizzo T-shirts and dads with Ryno T-shirts, and grandpa is still wearing that Ernie shirt. That's a statement that not every organization can make. Granted, we're 3 for 150 or whatever, but, hey, it's better than zero. For Cub fans, it's like a gravy that they like to pour on everything. They don't mind the whole story. The long, drawn-out drought of not winning, now that that's over. It's just really a cool story and being a part of that folklore is what makes it so unique. That faithful generational fan shouldn't be under-estimated, and it shouldn't be under-valued."

35. Gene Hiser

Gene Hiser played for the Chicago Cubs as an outfielder during five seasons between 1971 and 1975. He described himself in a telephone interview as "an old school baseball guy. Numbers don't mean a thing to me. Sometimes you're just trying to score a run, not think about your stats."

There was one number, however, that was always on the minds of the team's fans, and thus mattered to Hiser very much. When he joined the club in 1971, the figure was "63" and it rose one digit higher each year until it topped out at "108" in 2016. The number in question was of course, the counter of Cub seasons without a World Series victory. Long after his retirement from professional baseball, Hiser heard the same question over and over again from anxious die-hards: "When will the Cubs win it all?"

Finally after 108 years, extra innings and the most excruciating 17-minute rain delay in recorded history, the question was definitively answered. Hiser felt more than joy. He also experienced a sense of weight lifting from his shoulders. Of the 2016 World Series championship, he said, "It was the greatest thing. And I was also excited that I wouldn't be asked anymore if the Cubs would ever win. I was so glad that victory took that question out of circulation."

Hiser, who volunteers his time with Chicago Baseball Cancer Charities (CBCC), was not born a citizen of Cubs

Nation. As a boy in Baltimore, Maryland Hiser was raised in a family with divided baseball loyalties. He said:

"I grew up an Orioles fan. My mother was a Yankees fan, and my grandfather was a Boston supporter. My grandpa played semi-pro ball with Babe Ruth before ultimately becoming a brick layer. He was the head contractor for the build of Baltimore Memorial Stadium, which was almost entirely brick.

Because of his work on the park, I walked on the field before almost anyone else did. I'd get picked up from kindergarten and we'd go to Memorial Stadium."

These early experiences absorbing the sights and smells of the field combined with a whole lot of winning to cement Hiser's Baltimore fandom. He said of the team's run through the late 1960s, deep into the 1970s:

"The Orioles were something else. They were amazing. We got guys like Hall of Famers Brooks Robinson and Jim Palmer and we were winning the World Series. We were great for years."

The Cubs were actually a winning team when Hiser was selected by the club in the first round of the 1970 draft. However legions of fans were still smarting from the spectacular collapse of the 1969 season. They were paying attention as the new kid took the field for the franchise's centennial in 1971. Hiser said:

"At the time I was drafted, I knew almost nothing about

the Cubs. They were in the National League, and I had to buy the *Sporting News* to get caught up on the rest. I knew the guys that were All-Stars, like Ernie Banks and Fergie Jenkins, but not much else.

"It was a huge learning experience for me, but not for the fans. They knew who I was. They knew everything. At the time, there was something like five newspapers in the area and everybody who came to the park was informed. They expected our best. The reputation was that Cub fans were just partiers. They partied of course, but they knew the game. They knew who you were even without your name on the back. When they didn't like you, you heard it loud and clear."

Although the Cubs were still one of the top teams in baseball when Hiser arrived in Chicago, as his career progressed, he said, "there weren't that many people coming to Wrigley Field." The lack of crowds rather counterintuitively fostered a deeper connection between players and the public that Hiser views as unique and special, a feature of natural camaraderie offered by the Friendly Confines. Of his former workplace, Hiser said:

"It's a gorgeous place. Once the ivy grows in each season, it's just beautiful inside. In my playing days, it was neat because you were able to get really close to the people. The stands were open when we took batting practice. You'd have four or five guys hit for 15 minutes. When you were hitting, other guys were signing autographs. The bleachers were right there next to the left field line. And pitchers would be sitting on the fence with people right behind them. We'd do sprints in the outfield and sign autographs against the fence."

Hiser was continually amazed by the dedicated fans inside the park, as well as by those who took to the road. He remarked, "We would have so many people at our hotels when we traveled, people would stick with us for six or seven games. You'd see a lot of the same people all of the time".

The one-time Cubs outfielder has troves of unforgettable memories from his playing days. He reflected on a few:

"My first start in the big leagues, I hit against Bob Gibson and Fergie was pitching for the Cubs. The game only lasted an hour and 20 minutes. Great pitching, not much run scoring. My first hit came off reliever Mike Marshall and my only home run was against the Mets off Buzz Capra in a tight game."

But what Hiser remembers most, with heartfelt gratitude, was the support (and sometimes disapproval) of Cubs fans. The fans he said "were always with you. They were good to you and it made it easy to be good to them."

36. Stewart McVicar

Like so many Cub fans across the country, media personality and philanthropist Stewart McVicar first became aware of the team through the reach of television superstation WGN. However, the discovery was completely accidental. In a telephone interview, McVicar described the childhood moment that would permanently change the course of his life:

"Whatever I was into as a kid, I was pretty passionate about it. I was a big Superman fan and loved the cartoon, which was on Channel 9 [WGN-TV] back then. I went to turn on the show one day, but it was a Cubs game instead."

After recovering from brief disappointment, the founder of the Club 400 venue, charitable foundation and podcast found himself mesmerized by another type of superhero – one with big glasses, a microphone and a booming voice. He said:

"All of the sudden I hear an old guy say, 'There's a drive down the line…one run is in…two runs are in, and here's another runner coming around third…Here's the throw… He is safe!' I wondered, 'What is this guy so excited about?' Harry Caray's passion and love for the game radiated out of the TV, and into my soul.

"He is still my idol. When his health went downhill, it killed me. Harry loved baseball. He loved to have a good time. He was the life of the party and it changed the Cubs – and me – forever."

After that first Caray experience, McVicar was hooked and his passion for the Cubs became a family affair, though he was "someone who had neither seen nor played baseball, and didn't know the rules." Fortunate in having a supportive mother and grandparents, outings and vacations quickly became centered on the game. "My mom started taking us to Wrigley Field and then there were road trips, like one to Pittsburgh to watch the Cubs play the Pirates," he said.

It was during one of these baseball tours that McVicar began to understand the larger meaning of "family" as it applies to the global community of Cub fans. In Cincinnati to visit Riverfront Stadium (replaced by the Great American Ball Park in 2003), he and his kin encountered another group of die-hards nicknamed The Wild Bunch. This unapologetically loud, beer-guzzling gang frequently convened at Bernie's, a well-known watering hole in Wrigleyville on Clark Street. McVicar described an urban legend surrounding the club's name, "Rumor has it that one day, the Cubs suffered an extra tough loss. Someone walked into the bar, saw the sad faces and heard the silence and said 'Wow, what a wild bunch.'"

The Wild Bunch frequently took the fun (and misery) on the road. McVicar said that in Cincinnati, "My mom met some women, got to talking and the rest is history. We have lifelong friendships with some people to this day." One of those long-running relationships is with Dorothy Farrell, a legendary 92-year-old fan as well known to Wrigley Field regulars as Ronnie "Woo Woo" Wickers and Jerry Pritikin, "The Bleacher Preacher." McVicar said that Farrell is "like a grandmother to me."

Before turning his lifelong passion for the Cubs into philanthropic work with Club 400, a Lake in the Hills shrine to fandom that occupies 2,300 square feet – the entirety of his home's basement – a younger McVicar tried earning a living as a Wrigley T-shirt vendor. It was through this experience that he came to appreciate the advice of a fellow seller, who after a particularly tough day observed, "Stewart, you'll be better off just being a fan."

When a fire in McVicar's Wrigleyville apartment pushed him back home with his family in suburban McHenry County, the man behind the famous "We Got Wood" shirts of the late 1990s left his entrepreneur days with the neighborhood. But he never abandoned the Cubs. McVicar hasn't missed a home opener by his own estimation, "since like 1987," and attends roughly 50 games each season. When asked what keeps him coming back, what motivates him to make the up to 4-hour round trip from his home to The Friendly Confines, McVicar didn't hesitate:

"It's the community. I go to dozens of Cubs games every year. I went faithfully during seasons when I pretty much knew they were going to lose. But when you go to the game, you are part of another family. There are certain people you always see, the ushers and peanut guy. It's like *Cheers*. Everybody knows your name. It's all about the people. It's what makes the experience so special."

Though McVicar considers himself just a regular fan, not every blue bleeder regularly entertains Cub superstars. Club 400 has hosted charity events with partners such as former pitcher Kerry Wood, and 2017 Roberto Clemente Award-winner Anthony Rizzo. In 2019, the ultimate fan cave will welcome 2016 World Series MVP Ben Zobrist, and 2018's National League All-Star catcher Willson Contreras.

For all the opportunities, joy and heartbreak Cub fandom has bestowed upon McVicar, he described feeling curiously calm when the ultimate dream came to fruition in 2016. He said, "I always wondered how I would feel when the Cubs won the World Series. When it happened, all I felt was relief, like I was un-constipated for the first time in years. My life was complete."

A new era where the Chicago Cubs are the Lovable Losers no more hasn't diminished McVicar's awe of the team, and its borderless nation of fans. Each season brings new thrills. "The Cubs are universal," he said. "It's an ideal that will never change."

37. Rich Nye

Rich Nye is a modern-day Renaissance man. Drafted by the Chicago Cubs in 1966 while a civil engineering student at the University of California, Berkeley, the left-handed pitcher threw five seasons of Major League Baseball before moving onto other noteworthy careers in construction engineering (working on Chicago's Willis Tower), commodities trading and veterinary medicine. In his limited free time, the Chicago Baseball Cancer Charities (CBCC) supporter also creates beautiful woodwork. When asked about his professional diversity in a telephone interview, Nye said:

"I played baseball. I got to put on my glove, go out on the field and run around. When doing what you love, it doesn't matter if you get knocked out. You get paid to play and have fun. I had this engineering degree but it wasn't something that I got up in the morning and was excited to do. But baseball and working in the animal field give me that joy. I've enjoyed 40 plus years of following my passions."

Woodworking, a more recent venture, has offered Nye opportunities to unite two of his favorite hobbies. In 2010, when former Cub outfielder Andre Dawson was inducted into the Hall of Fame, Nye and some his fellow "old timers" signed a bat he handcrafted and presented it to Dawson as a gift. Nye has enjoyed many, diverse career highs. But there's a special place in his heart for the achievements he garnered as a young baseball player.

Nye was recognized by sportswriters as Chicago's Rookie of the Year in 1968, and credits his older brother for putting him on a path that ultimately led to Wrigley Field. He said:

"My brother was my influence in so many ways. He was approaching Lttle League play at age 11, a fairly tall, young fellow, strong, athletic. He took a position as a catcher and needed me to play catch with him so he could work on his skills. I had a glove and of course liked to play baseball, but it wasn't yet a passion."

That quickly changed. Nye continued:

"My brother gave me some throwing challenges to help get him into shape. He got me on the mound, and eventually I was able to throw - and able to throw strikes. My grandfather was watching us one day and said, 'Man, [Rich] is a natural.' It was an epiphany. I loved the game."

The Oakland, California native was not born a Cub man. His mother was a die-hard San Francisco Giants fan. Nye said, "She loved Willie Mays and so did I. We had the game on whenever it was broadcast."

The co-founder of the Midwest Bird and Exotic Animal Hospital in Westchester, Illinois reported that his "familiarity with the Cubs and Cub history came when a scout approached me about the 1966 draft." Nye had already secured summer employment on a survey crew in the San Francisco East Bay, planning to leverage his civil engineering studies. However he didn't hesitate long before accepting the Cubs' offer. Rather humbly he reported, "I had an opportunity and an education to fall back on. There was no downside. My brother and father thought I should give it a shot. It couldn't hurt."

The left-hander quickly made an impression and was called up to the big leagues. According to Nye, the mid-1960s was the perfect time for a young, ambitious kid to walk onto Wrigley Field. He said:

"I don't think I could have put myself in a better spot than joining the Cubs when they were at the absolute bottom, 10th in the National League. We had a young pitching staff, players and four future Hall of Famers on the team. This experience mixed with our young energy, it was just exciting to go into the ballpark every day. The fans started going crazy, lining up in 1967 at 10 am to get into the park and sit in the bleachers. By mid-summer, we were pushing toward first place. This excitement from the fans and the fact that we were battling for something for a change, it was such an energizer."

Naturally, the agonizing defeat that came of the 1969 season left a mark on Nye and his teammates. He credited the fans for driving the energy of that year, and for pulling the team through tough times:

"During the long period of the Lovable Losers, people always wanted to get behind us and support us. In '67, when we started to win, it was amazing how many people showed commitment. Nine- to 12-year-old kids could get into the park cheaply. They'd line up around the block cheering. Those kids are the die-hards that exist today, the fans who celebrated the 2016 World Series win with so much emotion. It's never about the money for the fans. It was always the ring, being champions."

Though he retired from Major League Baseball in 1970 after his final mound appearance for the Montreal Expos, Nye experienced a player's euphoria when the Cubs finally won it all in 2016. When asked to describe his feelings about the World Series victory, Nye said:

"It was a rocket booster. Game 7 of the World Series, I sat in the living room by myself. One of my boys was in California and texting me. I was on the edge of my seat. My wife would come in to check on me when I collapsed after a tougher moment. The emotions were just amazing. When they finally won it, I felt proud to be part of the Cubs organization, and to still feel part of it. I never felt that same connection with other teams I played for."

Like so many famous names interviewed for this book, Nye assigned all responsibility for the close Cub family culture to the team's legions of fans. He said, "I'm still Facebook friends with my fan club president from all those years ago when she was just a young high school student. These relationships have a new energy from the Cubs being competitive every year. Winning wasn't a fluke. We are part of the conversation every year now. It's a huge and amazing shift – and the fans deserve it."

38. Jeff Santo

Ask Jeff Santo how big a part of his life the Cubs were when he was growing up in Glenview, just outside of Chicago. The question is met first with a chuckle. Then a long pause.

"That's a big question," said Santo, one of three children born to Cubs Hall of Famer Ron Santo. "My brother [Ron Jr.] and I were born right into it. My dad was called up to the big leagues in 1960. My brother was born in '61 and I was born in '63. For the rest of my childhood – ten years – it was being at Wrigley Field. Those memories are so powerful. Looking back, it was such a unique childhood. We didn't know any different, because that was our world. In the summer going to the games with my dad, going in the locker room…I can almost retrace my steps as a kid because they were so vivid back then. That time for me was so powerful and so vivid that when it ended, it was almost like – wow, it's over – that world is gone. You don't realize how tough that is to deal with. You don't realize until after a while that that world kind of went away from us. It was such a family and it was so strong."

His father played for the Cubs from 1960 to 1973 before ending his career in 1974 with the cross-town White Sox. He was a nine-time All-Star with a .277 batting average, hit 342 home runs and batted in 1,331 runs. He won five Gold Gloves. He was one of the two defining third basemen, along with Baltimore's Brooks Robinson, of the 1960s.

In 1990, Santo became a radio broadcaster, teaming with veteran Pat Hughes at WGN. The pair were an oddly perfect fit with Hughes playing the straight man to Santo's everyman. On the air, Santo became the voice for all long-suffering Cubs fans, wearing his emotions firmly on his sleeve. In his voice, the fans heard the joys and the disappointments as they experienced them, mixed in with good-natured storytelling and self-deprecating humor – oftentimes about his hairpiece mishaps – during the inevitable down times.

Jeff Santo said his father was much like he was on the field and later in the broadcast booth. "He was intense, but he was fun. If he wasn't in a good mood, you stayed away from him…He took the game home. When they won, it was great. When they lost, well, let's just say that he was all baseball."

His father's story is well-known to any true Cubs fan. A statue of him stands outside of Wrigley Field, at the corner of Sheffield and Addison, alongside his longtime teammate and fellow Hall of Famer Billy Williams. The statue was dedicated on August 10, 2010; Santo died less than four months later, on December 3, 2010, from complications of diabetes, the disease he'd battled for much of his life and in secret through most of his playing days.

The younger son tells that story in a moving film called "This Old Cub" that chronicles his dad's courageous fight against all of the ailments that ganged up on him from decades of battling diabetes, from the hardship of having both legs amputated to the cancer that infected his bladder.

After playing college baseball at Miami of Ohio, Jeff Santo turned to screenwriting and filmmaking. He moved to Los Angeles, where he made his debut independent film, "Liar's Poker," in 1997.

Then the devastating toll that diabetes had taken on his dad hit like a punch to the gut. In December 2001, his father had his right leg amputated. That's when he thought about turning the camera on his father.

"I said to my mom, this would just be a great story to tell – what he's gone through, what he's going through – and that's when it hit me: I know how to write, and I know how to tell a story. So, the first thing I had to do was ask my dad if he wants to do this, and I remember going to him as he was waiting to go to surgery on the second leg. I told him what I possibly wanted to do. He got a little nervous. I told him it would touch a lot of people, that no one knows what you're going through and what you'd gone through and all that you'd accomplished. He said, 'Let's give it two weeks and if I don't like what's going on, we're done.' I said, 'All right.' The two weeks went by and he never said we're done. That's how that went. From there, I just followed him, and the process just happened."

After the second leg was amputated in December 2002, the film intimately captures what his father dealt with on a day-to-day basis as he learned to live with his prostheses. "That was tough, but when I turned on that camera, he turned it up a notch, like [Sandy] Koufax was pitching or something," Santo said. "So, it almost helped him through it in a way."

The original version of the documentary came out in 2004 and it shows the disappointment that came when Santo was first passed over by the Hall of Fame's veterans committee in 2003. A new edition was released in 2011, a year after he died, when the Hall's veterans committee finally voted him in. It shows Jeff's younger sister, Judy, answering the phone call, and the joy and relief that came with it. "That was pure joy," he said, "because we had so many go the other way. It was pure joy and wishing that he was there but knowing that he was in some way there with us and that he'd be [in the Hall of Fame] forever now."

Jeff's father of course never got to see the one thing that he wanted more than anything: the Cubs winning the World Series. That wouldn't come until six years after his death. Jeff was at Game 5 of the World Series at Wrigley Field, which the Cubs won 3-2 to stay alive. "We were at 5, and that was the family – my wife, my sister, my two nephews and my brother – and we had the best time of our lives. It was just so magical – we couldn't even believe we were there."

For Game 7, Jeff and his wife, Christie, were in the middle of a move from Arizona to Los Angeles the next day.

"I don't know what I was thinking, moving the next day…it was stupid. We had the patio furniture and a TV, and that's it – that's how we watched Game 7. When they won, we went nuts."

Soon after, WGN's Andy Masur called for his reaction. "That was kind of tough," he said. "There was just a lot of emotion…The whole thing."

Jeff and his wife have moved back to Los Angeles to try to develop TV shows. The two of them have a couple of things in the works but there's one that he calls his "passion project." The working title is *Blue Collar Famous*, and it's about a baseball player and his family life in the Golden Era of Baseball, when players had to hold second jobs and negotiated one-year contracts.

"It's a fictional story," he said, "but it's based on my dad and our family. The dad has a secret illness that his wife and him keep from the organization and the public, and how they maintain that.

"Back then, to be able regulate his diabetes with one shot in the morning and to be on the field for the rest of the day with no glucometers and to play 15 years and to endure all those games in the summer and to never miss a game – maybe a half a dozen in the sixties…that part of this was really interesting to me. It's about the relationship between the player and the wife and how they survive."

Sounds like a winning story if ever there was one.

The Authors

Becky Sarwate is is a freelance writer contributing to a number of publications including *The Broadway Blog*, where she reviews Chicago theater productions, and *Wrigleyville Nation*, chronicling the highs and lows of lifelong Chicago Cubs fandom. Becky also publishes a political/cultural column for *Contemptor* and has written for PoliticusUSA.com, *RootSpeak* magazine, *NewCity*, *Make It Better*, and *StreetWise*. She has been recognized eight times by the National Federation of Press Women for excellence in communications.

As an adjunct member of Northeastern Illinois University's English department faculty, Sarwate realizes a passion for educating and mentoring the next generation of communicators. Sarwate was also the 49th President of the Illinois Woman's Press Association, founded in 1885 and remains on the Executive Board as Immediate Past President/Digital Marketing Chair.

Sarwate is a proud city of Chicago resident, where she lives in the Ravenswood neighborhood with her husband Bob. Her collected works can be found at BeckySarwate.com.

An attorney and award-winning journalist, **Randy Richardson** is a founding member and first president of the nonprofit Chicago Writers Association. He is the first male recipient of the National Federation of Press Women's Communicator of Achievement Award. His essays have been published in the anthologies *Chicken Soup for the Father and Son Soul*, *Humor for a Boomer's Heart*, *The Big Book of Christmas Joy*, and *Cubbie Blues: 100 Years of Waiting Till Next Year*, as well as in numerous print and online journals. He is the author of two novels, *Cheeseland* and *Lost in the Ivy*, both from Eckhartz Press.

A die-hard Cubs fan, Randy is a regular contributor to *Wrigleyville Nation*. He lives a Purple Line Express away from Wrigley Field with his wife Mitsuko, their son Tyler, and their two cats, Smokey and Bandit. Read more about him at lostintheivy.com and cheeselandthebook.com.

Charity Partners

The authors have partnered with and are donating 100 percent of their proceeds from book sales to two charities: Chicago Baseball Cancer Charities (CBCC) and Club 400. CBCC helps fund cancer research and patient care programs at Chicago-area hospitals, and supporting services to empower kids with cancer. Club 400's mission statement is simple: "Cubs fans helping Cubs fans." Both are federally-registered 501(c)(3) tax-deductible charitable organizations.

Cubsessions

is available at:
www.eckhartzpress.com

ECKHARTZ PRESS

Also available on Eckhartz Press:

- *The Living Wills* by Rick Kaempfer & Brendan Sullivan
- *Chasing the Lost City* by Tom Weinberg
- *Safe Inside* by Lee Kingsmill
- *Turn it Up!* by Bob Shannon
- *Doin' the Cruise* by Mitch Michaels w/ Ken Churilla
- *Everything I Know I Learned from Rock Stars* by Bill Paige
- *I Had a Runny Nose* by Tom Latourette
- *Genuflections* by Robert Herguth
- *GelSrong* by Mark Gelinas
- *We Have Company* by Bobby Skafish
- *Patty and the Stump* by Manton Clue
- *Out the Door!* by M.L. Collins
- *In Small Boxes* by Ann Wilson
- *Rantings of a Bitter Childless Woman* by Jeanne Bellezzo
- *Monkey in the Middle* by Dobie Maxwell
- *Grun Weiss Vor!* By Rick Kaempfer and Todd "Fritz" Schneider
- *Hugh Hefner's First Funeral and Other True Tales of Love and Death in Chicago* by Pat Colander
- *Brandwidth* by Kipper McGee
- *Truffle Hunt* by Brent Petersen
- *Father Knows Nothing* by Rick Kaempfer
- *Back in the Game* by Rich King and Lindsay Eanet